John Colet

THE HISTORY OF THE GERMAN
LABOUR MOVEMENT

Helga Grebing

THE HISTORY OF THE GERMAN LABOUR MOVEMENT

A Survey

Abridged by Mary Saran
Translated by Edith Körner

BERG PUBLISHERS

Published in German in 1966
by Nymphenburger Verlagshandlung, Munich
© 1969 for the English edition
Oswald Wolff (Publishers) Ltd., London

This revised edition published 1985 by
Berg Publishers Ltd.,
24 Binswood Avenue, Leamington Spa,
Warwickshire CV32 5SQ
51 Washington Street, Dover,
New Hampshire 03820, USA

British Library Cataloguing in Publication Data

Grebing, Helga
The history of the German labour movement: a survey.—[2nd] ed.
1. Labour and labouring classes—Germany—History
I. Title   II. Saran, Mary   III. Geschichte der Deutschen
Arbeiterbehegung. *English*
335′.00943   HD6694

ISBN 0-907582-29-X
ISBN 0-907582-31-1 Pbk

Library of Congress Cataloging in Publication Data

Grebing, Helga.
  The history of the German labour movement.

  Translation of: Geschichte der deutschen Arbeiterbewegung.
  Bibliography: p.
  Includes index.
  1. Labor and laboring classes—Germany—History.
I. Saran, Mary. II. Title.
HD8448.G713 1985   331.88′0943   84 – 73483
ISBN 0 – 907582 – 29 – X
ISBN 0 – 907582 – 31 – 1 (pbk.)

Printed in Great Britain by
Billing & Sons Limited, Worcester

CONTENTS

AUTHOR'S PREFACE TO THE ENGLISH EDITION

My purpose in writing this book was to present a comprehensive survey of the history of the German labour movement in its various manifestations in the general context of social and political development. In order to indicate the kind of information which the reader may expect to find in this work, I shall briefly outline the most important historical phases whose political, sociological, economic, psychological and ideological aspects are later described in detail.

The change from a feudal agrarian system with its peasant and craft economy to the bourgeois epoch of industrial capitalism saw the initially very modest beginnings of the labour movement in Germany, together with the emergence of the first social theories which, in the middle of the nineteenth century, culminated in the works of Karl Marx and Friedrich Engels.

The militant, class-conscious character of the German proletariat became pronounced only after 1870, when the social consequences of the foundation of the Empire made themselves felt; it was then that the revolutionary theories of Marx and Engels became widely accepted and that the German labour movement created the mighty organization which—though never realizing its full power-potential in Germany itself—dominated the Second International.

The revolution of 1918 remained, as far as the labour movement was concerned, incomplete: though it transformed the monarchic, authoritarian state into a democratic, parliamentary republic which offered incomparably greater scope to the labour movement, the ruling classes of the Empire continued to dominate the social and economic scene. The end of the war also brought with it the split between Socialists and Communists, which had long been smouldering in the labour movement and now became irreversible.

By accepting the Weimar Republic in principle as a basis for the realization of its social and political goals, the social-democratic movement became the implacable opponent of all the radical groups whose aim was to replace parliamentary democracy by a dictatorship of the Right or the Left.

After 1945 the social-democratic labour movement gradually, and with many reversals, discarded its traditional revolutionary theory. In accordance with the changes in the social structure of the population in the Federal Republic the Social Democratic Party has changed from a closed party representing a specific class into a party seeking to appeal to and represent various sections of the population. The SPD's programme is based on ethical values and a belief in the pluralistic society. It is directed towards a socially progressive and liberal policy, identifying itself with the state and depending for its realization in the main on a pragmatic approach. As a result of this process of change in the party, the task of representing the specifically working-class interests outside parliament falls now predominantly to the trade unions.

During the chequered history of the labour movement set-backs, failures, mistakes and inadequacies have at times hampered and retarded—on occasions virtually frustrated—the realization of its objectives. Yet the movement has invariably shown itself strong enough to resume its tasks under changed circumstances.

The English edition of this book will, I hope, serve the same purpose as I had in mind when addressing the German reader: firstly, it may prove a useful introduction for those interested in history and politics who wish to learn something about the German labour movement before proceeding to a more detailed study of the subject; secondly, it may furnish material for those who are directly involved in politics and who may find in the development of the German labour movement a—positive or negative—yardstick for their own actions.

H.G.

AUTHOR'S POSTSCRIPT

The manuscript for the German edition of this book was completed in autumn 1965. Since then the political alignments determined by the outcome of the Second World War have been subject to change all over the world. The citizens of the Federal Republic became aware of this general flux only when the end of the so-called economic miracle and the onset of the 1966 recession gave a new urgency to the question about cause and effect and, by implication, about contents and aims of politics in the Federal Republic.

In December 1966 the leading bodies of the SPD decided in favour of the party joining the CDU/CSU in a Great Coalition. They took this step in order to combat the recession, to carry out the urgently needed reform of the country's finances, to pass the emergency legislation which had for a whole decade been the cause of much contention, and, above all, to bring about a long overdue re-orientation of the policy towards the East. However, a Great Coalition had in any case been a long cherished conception of the party. The decision was, and has remained, controversial both inside and outside the SPD. The opponents of the Great Coalition see in it yet another danger threatening a still imperfectly developed democracy; they fear that it may encourage the tendency— which has been in evidence for a long time—towards a plebiscitary authoritarian régime. While these fears are not without substance, it must be admitted that the Great Coalition has been able to stem the recession sufficiently for unemployment figures to drop. Furthermore, the Chairman of the SPD, Willy Brandt, who holds the offices of Deputy-Chancellor and Foreign Minister, deserves the main credit for the far more flexible foreign policy the Federal Republic is now pursuing.

The Great Coalition has been an important contributory factor in the development of a relatively broadly-based extra-parliamentary opposition. Since the adoption of the Godesberg Programme in 1959, there had been a continuous change in the nature and image of the SPD : from a closed party engaged in a continuous effort to integrate the several conflicting interests of various sections of the population, to a party of the whole population proclaiming the harmonious reconciliations of a supposed community of interests. The fears aroused by this development were confirmed : on the political Left, forces tending towards a radical-democratic, socialist viewpoint, became unattached, no longer being attracted to any political party. Their eventual integration will be possible only by long-sustained efforts for a *rapprochement* on both sides.

These forces, however, no longer come—at any rate not predominantly—from the sociological strata which used to provide recruits for the radical Left. For it was neither the long-established small Left-wing groupings nor the illegal KPD who benefited by the opposition to the Great Coalition; the initiative for a new political movement and for breaking through fossilized social structures came from the students' movement, inspired by the SDS. It is far too early to say whether this students' movement, as its representatives believe, will be able to create a viable basis for a renewal of Socialism or whether it will eventually exhaust itself in protests against the technological society and its culture, protests which are nourished by an anarchist mood. In any case, there are as yet no signs whatsoever of any willingness on the part of the Left-wing workers to act in solidarity with the students' movement.

On the other hand, the sceptical and even negative attitude towards the Great Coalition within the SPD has brought about a revival of internal democracy in the party; frequently, the initiative for this has come from sections of the trade unions. Nearly a thousand critical or challenging resolutions were submitted to the SPD's Congress held in Nuremberg in March 1968. At that Congress, questions which had long been considered taboo or put into cold storage were discussed, e.g. the recognition of the Oder-Neisse line or the demand for an extension of co-determination. The party was manifestly searching for a new image. The party leadership (the place of Fritz Erler, who had died in 1967, was taken by Helmut Schmidt, born 1918, the chairman of the parliamentary party) did not resist this move though it did not help to promote it. However, Willy Brandt was confirmed as party leader, and he is accepted as the representative of the whole party.

Whether the unrest in the party continues and whether it can be made fruitful will depend on internal and external factors : on the results of the Federal election of 1969 and on the repercussions of world events on the German Federal Republic.

H.G.

20 June 1968.

ABBREVIATIONS

ADAV	*Allgemeiner Deutscher Arbeiterverein*	
	German General Workers' Association	
ADGB	*Allgemeiner Deutscher Gewerkschaftsbund*	
	General Confederation of German Trade Unions	
AFA-Bund	*Allgemeiner Freier Angestelltenbund*	
	General Free Confederation of Salaried Employees	
BGL	*Betriebsgewerkschaftsleitung*	
	Workshop Trade Union Council	
CDU	*Christlich-demokratische Union*	
	Christian Democratic Union	
CSU	*Christlich-soziale Union*	
	Christian Social Union	
CGB	*Christliche Gewerkschaftsbewegung*	
	Christian Trade Union Movement	
Comintern	Communist International	
DAF	*Deutsche Arbeitsfront*	
	German Labour Front	
DAG	*Deutsche Angestelltengewerkschaft*	
	German Salaried Employees' Union	
EEC	European Economic Community	
FDGB	*Freier Deutscher Gewerkschaftsbund*	
	Free German Trade Union Confederation (after 1919)	
FDGB	after 1945, same name and initials for communist trade union organization	
IG	*Industriegewerkschaft*	
	Industrial Union	
IJB	*Internationaler Jugend-Bund*	
	International League of Youth	
ISK	*Internationaler Sozialistischer Kampf-Bund*	
	Militant Socialist International	
KAPD	*Kommunistische Arbeiterpartei Deutschlands*	
	Communist Workers' Party of Germany	

KPD	*Kommunistische Partei Deutschlands*
	Communist Party of Germany
KPO	*Kommunistische Partei Opposition*
	Communist Party Opposition
NATO	North Atlantic Treaty Organization
NSDAP	*Nationalsozialistische Deutsche Arbeiterpartei*
	National Socialist German Workers' Party
SAP	*Sozialistische Arbeiterpartei*
	Socialist Workers' Party
SDS	*Sozialistischer Deutscher Studentenbund*
	German Socialist Students' League
SED	*Sozialistische Einheitspartei Deutschlands*
	Socialist Unity Party of Germany
SPD	*Sozialdemokratische Partei Deutschlands*
	Social Democratic Party of Germany
USPD	*Unabhängige Sozialdemokratische Partei Deutschlands*
	Independent Social Democratic Party of Germany
WWI	*Wirtschaftswissenschaftliches Institut*
	Institute for Economic Research (of the trade unions)

CHAPTER I

1800–1850

1. *Social and Economic Conditions before 1850*

In Germany, like everywhere else in Europe, the exceptionally rapid growth of the population constituted an essential factor in the development of the economic and social conditions in the nineteenth century.

Assuming the frontiers of 1914, the population figures for Germany were as follows (in millions): 1800 24·5; 1830 29·6; 1850 35·4; 1870 40·8; 1890 49·5; 1910 64·9; 1914 67·8; 1925 67·4 (excluding Alsace-Lorraine); they had thus increased two and a half times within 125 years. Between 1816 and 1845, the number of inhabitants rose by 38·7 per cent (from 24·8 millions to 34·4 millions).

There were various causes for this increase of population in Germany: falling mortality figures due to improved hygiene, more advanced methods of medical treatment, and a more sensible and varied diet. The same reasons caused the birthrate to rise as infant mortality fell. In urban, though not in rural areas, this trend was reversed after 1900.

The population explosion made itself especially felt in the country, more particularly in the Eastern rural regions of Prussia; it was associated with the emancipation of the serfs (in Prussia between 1807 and 1850). The reforms in Prussia stipulated that the peasants, whose conditions had hitherto been one of serfdom, should surrender up to half of their land to the lord of the manor as compensation for personal services which they would no longer have to perform, for duties in kind, and for being allowed to hold their property without restrictions. At a later stage it became possible to discharge this obligation in cash. As a result of these regulations, the remaining or mortgaged land in many cases no longer provided a living for the peasants; they often lived for decades on the very borderline of subsistence, hardly able to profit from their personal freedom. Only gradually did they learn to accept new, more rational production methods, and to exploit the opportunities of the modern money economy, though in some cases they sold their property, which was no longer profitable, to the landlord, and became, at best, his tenants. But the smallholders, who had been excluded from the reforms, often had no alternative but to hand over their property to the landlord in exchange for their freedom, and to become day-labourers in his employ.

Thus there came into being—principally in the rural Eastern parts of Prussia—below the stratum of large land-owners and an ultimately well-established class of farmers, a rural substratum : its members eked out a meagre living from their wage, their small allotment, an emaciated cow, some livestock, cottage crafts (in competition with the artisans, whose existence was already precarious), by collecting wood, begging and stealing. The working day increased to 12, 14 and 16 hours; both the women and the numerous children had to work. It was not till the onset of industrialization in the 'fifties that a demand for labour was created; in the 'sixties we see the rural labourers gradually drift from the East to the industrial centres of the West.

Apart from the peasant substratum, there existed in Germany, both in town and country, a substratum of artisans. The freedom of trade regulations (introduced in Prussia between 1806 and 1810, and only later in most other German states) did away with the strict mandatory obligation of guild membership which allowed only a privileged few to become master-craftsmen on whom the great mass of journeymen were dependent (the latter thus lacking the opportunity of building up an economic life of their own as a prerequisite for starting a family). As a result of the freeing of trade the number of independent craftsmen rose more rapidly than the population, and this led to an overcrowding of individual trades; in 1816 there were 30·8 masters and journeymen per 1,000 inhabitants, in 1861 the former figure rose to 59·0. In the main, these independent artisans worked at home for shops, warehouses and factories or they carried out repairs.

The genuinely independent craftsman could only hold his own against growing industrial competition by endlessly increasing the length of his working day, by sending his wife and children to work in the factories, or by living in the country on the vegetables, potatoes and fruit grown on his small allotment. Ultimately the craftsman—irrespective of whether he was master or journeyman—came to look upon the life of a factory worker as thoroughly desirable, since it kept him from sinking into the artisan proletariat.

But the worst destitution existed among the cottage workers —the weavers and spinners—of Silesia, Saxony, and Westphalia. Silesia in particular suffered such terrible misery that in the 'forties thousands died of typhus there. The major uprisings in Silesia—in Peterswaldau and Langenbielau in 1844—in protest against hunger and exploitation by merchants and middlemen were suppressed by the military. The hopelessness of the struggle of the craftsmen against rising competition from industry is reflected in the following figures : in 1837 there were 419 steam engines employed in Prussia; by 1849 this figure had risen to 1,444.

As we mentioned earlier, Germany had, up to 1850, made only fitful starts on industrialization. These comparatively slow beginnings were due to the tremendous capital losses suffered through war, pillage, and levies. Lack of capital and inadequate means of production confronted a surplus supply of labour. This was aggravated by the superiority of the English and French competitors in the textile, iron and mining industries. Entrepreneurs, many of whom had, prior to 1840, risen from among craftsmen, had first to learn the methods of rational production processes and then transmit them to the workers. Before 1850 many factories, particularly small ones, had a hard struggle to survive. The burden of this struggle was generally borne by the workers, whose social conditions continued to deteriorate : the working day was increased to 13 or 14, and in the 'forties to as much as 17 hours, and spent in appalling conditions; falling wages had to be made up by women and children going out to work, which in turn depressed wages further; incredible housing conditions and inadequate provisions against sickness, old age and accident were common.

Particularly humiliating for the worker was the so-called truck system. He had to use his wages to buy goods which he needed from his employer at inflated prices, or he received them in the form of goods which he did not need and which he had to re-sell to the employer at a reduced price so as to be able to buy necessities—again at inflated prices.

In only two areas did the state to some extent intervene against these abuses. The excessive physical demands imposed on children inhibited both their bodily and their mental development, so that in 1828 the Prussian general von Horn was forced to admit that "the factory areas are unable to furnish their complement to fill the ranks of the army . . .". But it was not till more than ten years later that the concern for the strength of the Prussian army led to the first piece of protective labour legislation : no children under nine were to be regularly employed in factories and mines; work at night and on Sundays and holidays was forbidden, and the working day limited to 10 hours. In 1849 Prussia and Saxony legislated against the truck system.

In 1853 further legislation in Prussia raised the minimum age for factory work to twelve years, and restricted the working hours for persons under fourteen to 7. In Saxony, however, factory work for children under ten was not forbidden till 1861. Only Saxony, Bavaria and Württemberg introduced some rather modest safety regulations. Women enjoyed no protection whatsoever. The control of the legal provisions was very lax, so that the laws could mostly be circumvented.

The first half of the nineteenth century was characterized in Germany by a gradual change-over from a rural and craft economy to an industrial one under the banner of economic and political liberalism. The different systems were still closely interlocked and this resulted in tensions and difficulties due to the need to adapt to new conditions. These difficulties were particularly rife among craftsmen, who, by the middle of the century, had split into master-craftsmen, keen to uphold the traditions and protectionism of the guilds, and journeymen, who were unable to improve their lot within the narrow and ossified confines of the organization; but neither group thought of itself as very far removed from the industrial proletariat.

The feelings of the hitherto still small class of factory workers were equally ambiguous. On the one hand they still felt the pull of the agrarian system of society in which land, house, family, and communal tasks played a determining role; on the other hand they had to contend with the contingencies of alternating booms and slumps, with the all-pervasive claims of the modern, entrepreneur-directed factory life, and with the work discipline to which they were subjected.

The factory owners were, on the one hand, still wedded to the paternalistic ideas of the guilds which they wanted to implement in the running of their factories; they were thus frequently in favour of some kind of welfare arrangements in their enterprises. On the other hand, for the sake of rising output, profitability, and stability, they mercilessly exploited their labour force, whom they regarded as a commodity.

The large landowners east of the Elbe, having profited from the Prussian land reform, enjoyed unequalled social and economic security. They had profited economically from the liberal economic policies of their state, and at the same time maintained the privileges of their estate.

The last decade before the outbreak of the 1848 revolution was as much characterized by the increasing prosperity of the few as by the growing poverty of the many.

2. Theories towards a Solution of Social Problems

The first theories towards the solution of social problems arising out of the changes in the political, social, and economic structure which followed upon the change of a feudal, agrarian system into an industrial bourgeois one, were developed in France and England, where the industrial revolution occurred earlier, and was both more rapid and more intensive. Saint-Simon, Fourier, Cabet, Lamennais, Blanc and Leroux in France, and Owen in England, formulated socialist, communist and anarchist theories and systems which—with varying intensity and to a different extent—influenced social criticism in Germany.

Thus e.g. the poet *Georg Büchner* (1813–1837), who in 1834 published the *"Hessische Landbote"*, was influenced by Lamennais and Leroux.

Wilhelm Weitling (1808–1871), regarded as the most distinctive German Socialist before 1848, was originally fired by a religious belief similar to that of Lamennais, whom—in spite of being a Protestant—he explicitly quoted; the influence of Saint-Simon, Fourier, Cabet and Owen can also be discerned in his writings. Weitling was a travelling tailor-journeyman. He shaped the political ideas of the League of the Just (which later became the Communist League) in Paris before Marx and Engels. He was highly esteemed among the German journeymen's associations, both in Paris and Switzerland.

Weitling's ideas aimed at a consistent, egalitarian Communism: the abolition of money, common ownership, equal standard of living for all, abolition of national frontiers, and the brotherhood of all men uniting them into a "family league of humanity". He repeatedly demanded immediate action and violent revolution. Yet he remained peculiarly attached to the craft-based order which was in process of dissolution. He thought more in terms of protecting the artisan and the small trader, of maintaining "the simple, harmonious life in towns and villages", and less in terms of industrialization and the proletariat. But it was just this outlook, allied to his naive religiosity, which allowed him to exercise such influence over the German journeymen abroad. Their social consciousness was not yet proletarian, and their social prestige was still determined by the ideas of the craftsman's estate. His influence among the German craft-associations declined after 1843, and in 1846, following a quarrel with Marx and Engels, he went to America. He returned briefly during the revolution of 1848. Back in America, he soon gave up politics altogether.

Moses Hess (1812–1875) was in sympathy with Weitling's early ideas. Hess was the first to speak of the socialist revolution as of the "last of all revolutions". He postulated rigidly ethical premisses for the creation of a communist society. He knew both Marx and Lassalle personally, and later worked as a publicist for the German labour movement.

Karl Marx was born in 1818 in Trier. His parents were descended from an old rabbinical family; in order to be allowed to practise law, his father became converted to Protestantism and in 1824 his children were also baptized.

Karl Marx studied in Bonn and Berlin. His main subject was philosophy, and he was awarded his doctorate in Jena in 1841. In 1842 he took over the editorship of the liberal *"Rheinische Zeitung"*, but after only six months as editor-in-chief he relinquished the post, and moved to Paris. "I can do nothing in Germany any more. One cannot be true to oneself here." Expelled from France in 1845, Marx lived in Brussels till 1848. His friendship with *Friedrich Engels* began in 1844 and was to last a life-time. Engels was born in Barmen in 1820, the son of a wealthy manufacturer, and was himself trained for business (i.a. in England). From 1845 till 1848 he lived with Marx in Brussels. Together they founded, in 1846, a Committee of Communist Corresponding Members. In 1847 they joined the League of the Just which shortly afterwards changed its name to Communist League. In December 1847 Marx was commissioned to formulate a "communist creed". The "Communist Manifesto", on which Engels collaborated, was completed in January 1848, and published in London where the League had its headquarters.

The Communist Manifesto contains ideas Marx had developed since the beginning of the 'forties, particularly in his "Critique of Hegel's Constitutional Law" (1843), the "Critique of Hegel's Philosophy of Law" (1843–44), and in the incomplete manuscripts (first published in 1931) of the "Critique of National Economy" (1844), "The Holy Family" (1844) and "German Ideology" (1845–46, jointly with Engels; first published in 1932). These writings were intended to define his own position, to join issue with the main works of English and French economists, and "to unmask the socialist and left-radical writers in Germany and Western Europe". Erroneously called "early writings", they give us an insight into Marx's motivation. It was not the case that Marx started as a philosopher who, in the course of his analysis in the "Capital", found that his real task was that of an economist, but rather that he was (and remained) a philosopher who had to become historian, economist and politician in order to grasp in its entirety man's situation in his time. Engels' painstaking empirical studies—his "The Condition of the Working Class in England" (published in 1845)—greatly strengthened the foundations of Marx's convictions.

The first part of the Communist Manifesto[1] about "Bourgeois and Proletarians" begins with the sentence : "The history of all hitherto existing society is the history of class struggles". This sentence represents the essence of Marx's and Engels' philosophy of history (which Engels later called the "materialist conception of history"); a detailed exposition of it can already be found in Marx's "German Ideology". At a later date Marx gave it an extremely pithy and clear formulation in the Preface to the "Contribution to the Critique of Political Economy" (1859)[2] :

> In the social production of their life, men enter into definite relations that are indispensable and independent of their will, relations of production which correspond to a definite stage of development of their material productive forces. The sum total of these relations of production constitutes the economic structure of society, the real foundations, on which rises a legal and political superstructure and to which correspond definite forms of social consciousness. The mode of production of material life conditions the social, political and intellectual life process in general. It is not the consciousness of men that determines their being, but, on the contrary, their social being that determines their consciousness.

Marx conceives the development of social conditions as a series of class struggles. Thus the ancient slave-owning state had slaves opposing the freemen who alone could claim rights and property; in mediaeval feudal society the physically and legally dependent peasant confronted the lord of the manor; later again the burghers, whose economic activities were restricted, stood against the absolute rule of the princes, till the French revolution gradually created a new society, one of bourgeois capitalism. This is what the Communist Manifesto has to say about it :

> Our epoch, the epoch of the bourgeoisie, possesses, however, this distinctive feature : it has simplified the class antagonism. Society as a whole is more and more splitting up into two great hostile camps, into two great classes directly facing each other : Bourgeoisie and Proletariat.

[1] "Karl Marx and Frederick Engels, Selected Works", Vol. I, Moscow, 1950.
[2] Ibid.

According to Marx (and Engels), the bourgeoisie "during its rule of scarce one hundred years, has created more massive and more colossal production forces than have all preceding generations together". But "not only has the bourgeoisie forged the weapons that bring death to itself; it has also called into existence the men who are to wield those weapons—the modern working class—the proletarians".

> In proportion as the bourgeoisie, i.e. capital, is developed, in the same proportion is the proletariat, the modern working class, developed—a class of labourers, who live only so long as they find work and who find work only so long as their labour increases capital. These labourers, who must sell themselves piecemeal, are a commodity, like every other article of commerce, and are consequently exposed to all the vicissitudes of competition, to all the fluctuations of the market.

In these words the Communist Manifesto sets out the thesis which Marx developed in his "Critique of National Economy", namely that "man's alienation from man" has brought about conditions in which man is completely lost in the proletariat.

How can this alienation of man, this subjection to alien forces, be overcome so that man can fashion the conditions under which he lives rather than be fashioned by them?

Marx answers that man will achieve self-realization only when the proletariat abolishes itself by its own exertions:

> When the proletariat announces the dissolution of the existing social order it only declares the secret of its own existence, for it constitutes the effective dissolution of this order.[1]

> The proletariat, on the contrary, is forced, as proletariat, to work for its own abolition of the condition which makes it a proletariat—private property.[2]

The conception that "the conditions of self-alienation . . . must at the same time be the conditions for the self-realization

[1] "Critique of Hegel's Philosophy of Law". From: "Karl Marx, Selected Writings in Sociology and Social Philosophy", London, 1956, pp. 182–3.
[2] "The Holy Family". From: "Karl Marx, Selected Writings in Sociology and Social Philosophy", London, 1956, p. 231.

of man" grew out of Marx's discussion and critical inversion of the Hegelian dialectic; it formed the basis of Marx's theory of the proletarian revolution. Marx's and Engels' lifelong, merciless and intransigent struggle to assert their doctrine, their "communist pride of infallibility" rested—if we disregard the psychological factors—on the conviction that their scientific insight into the economic structure of bourgeois society provides the only tenable theoretical basis for the emancipatory struggle of a self-alienated humanity.

Marx has not infrequently been interpreted as if his thought and work had been dominated by a profound tension, not easily reducible to a simple formula, between growth and form, evolution and revolution, the independent action of socio-economic forces and political freedom of action. The Communist Manifesto seems to confirm this.

On the one hand it enunciates its certainty about the future course of history, based on the understanding of historical interconnections:

> The development of Modern Industry, therefore, cuts from under its feet the very foundations on which the bourgeoisie produces and appropriates products. What the bourgeoisie, therefore, produces, above all, are its own grave-diggers. Its fall and the victory of the proletariat are equally inevitable.

On the other hand it calls for revolutionary action:

> The immediate aim of the Communists is the same as that of all the other proletarian parties: formation of the proletariat into a class, overthrow of the bourgeois supremacy, conquest of political power by the proletariat.

> The Communists disdain to conceal their views and aims. They openly declare that their ends can be attained only by the forcible overthrow of all existing social conditions. Let the ruling classes tremble at a Communist revolution. The proletarians have nothing to lose but their chains. They have a world to win. Working men of all countries, unite!

However, the question arises whether this interpretation does justice to Marx's seminal idea about the necessity of the dialectic unity of theory and practice.

The great goal which Marx and Engels set themselves was

to overcome man's self-alienation and to bring about his self-realization. This goal of genuine humanism (as Marx calls his own position) cannot be achieved by "raw Communism"; the negation of man's personality in every sphere seems to Marx to be the logical outcome of private ownership; it is the perfect expression of envy and of the levelling process. Thus Marx (and Engels) did not attack ownership as such, but the capitalist private ownership by the bourgeoisie of the socially important means of production. Their Communism therefore implies the abolition of exploitation by "the expropriation of the expropriators" and the socialization of the means of production :

> Communism is the positive abolition of private property, of human self-alienation, and thus, the real appropriation of human nature, through and for man. It is therefore the return of man himself as a social, that is, really human, being, a complete and conscious return which assimilates all the wealth of previous development. Communism, as a complete naturalism is humanism, and as a complete humanism is naturalism. It is the definitive resolution of the antagonism between man and Nature, and between man and man. It is the true solution of the conflict between existence and essence, between objectification and self-affirmation, between freedom and necessity, between individual and species. It is the solution of the riddle of history and knows itself to be this solution.[1]

But Communism is not the goal of history ("We give the name of Communism to a real movement which abolishes the existing state of affairs"—"German Ideology"); nor does it, for Marx, represent the fulfilment of the purpose of life. The goal is "the realization of man as man", and Communism is the condition if this purpose of life is to be achieved.

When we evaluate the achievements of Marx and Engels today, we should disregard the correctness or doubtfulness of their theories, the value or lack of value of their predictions, and above all the ideological and political misinterpretations of their ideas; instead, we should remember their "real humanism", their efforts to raise man from his position of "a humili-

[1] "Critique of National Economy". From: "Karl Marx, Selected Writings in Sociology and Social Philosophy", London, 1956, pp. 243–4.

ated, enslaved, abandoned and despicable being". It is impossible to overestimate the influence of Karl Marx's thought on the course of history and on all the social sciences.

Today, the confrontation with marxist ideas is a determining factor in the political thought and action not only in the industrialized, but—to an even greater extent—in the developing countries.

3. *The Beginnings of the Labour Movement in Germany*

Up to 1848 Germany, unlike England, had no labour movement. This was not primarily due to the fact that industrialization in Germany started later than in other countries of Western Europe, but rather because prior to 1848 the states of the German Confederation suppressed every kind of emancipatory agitation. While in England the Combination Laws were repealed in 1824–25, the proscription of political association and combination remained in full force in Germany up to the revolution of 1848. In addition, there was strict censorship. Though it has been shown that social self-help organizations among artisans, such as sick-benefit funds, distress funds and funeral insurance, existed since the beginning of the nineteenth century (and could be regarded as precursors of union activity), strikes can be traced as far back as the end of the eighteenth century : workers downed tools, striking journeymen left the cities, and there were some general strikes. From 1830 onwards, educational associations emerged, sometimes in collaboration with the liberal bourgeoisie, sometimes on the sole initiative of the journeymen and workers; they were devoted, in varying proportion, to the spread of knowledge and education, to discussions of current affairs and to conviviality.

The first signs of political activity evolved—secretly—in the educational associations of the travelling journeymen abroad : in France, Switzerland and England. The most important among them were a secret political association called New Germany, later renamed Young Germany, founded in Berne in 1834, and the Outlaws' Union, founded in Paris in the same year; the latter produced, in 1837, a splinter group, the League of the Just, whose programme and ideology were for some years under the influence of Wilhelm Weitling. After 1840 its centre of gravity shifted gradually from Paris to London—hence its well-known connection with Marx and Engels. At its London congress of 1847 the organization took the name of Communist League; its new statute, formulated during the second meeting in December 1847, already shows the influence of Marx and Engels; its first article states :

> The purpose of the League is the overthrow of the bourgeoisie, the rule of the proletariat, the abolition of the old bourgeois society which is based on class contradictions, and the creation of a new society without classes and privileges.

The Communist Manifesto appeared in London a few weeks before the revolution in Germany; it outlined in detail what the political activities of the members of the Communist League were to be :

> The Communists do not form a separate party opposed to other working-class parties. They have no interests separate and apart from those of the proletariat as a whole ...
>
> The Communists, therefore, are on the one hand, practically, the most advanced and resolute section of the working-class parties of every country, that section which pushes forward all others; on the other hand, theoretically, they have over the great mass of the proletariat the advantage of clearly understanding the line of march, the conditions and the ultimate general results of the proletarian movement ...
>
> In short, the Communists everywhere support every revolutionary movement against the existing social and political order of things. In all these movements they bring to the front, as the leading question in each, the property question, no matter what its degree of development at the time.
>
> Finally, they labour everywhere for the union and agreement of the democratic parties of all countries.

This shows that in Marx's and Engels' view the Communists, who were few in number, could not carry out a revolution; their task was to act within the framework of the massive movement of European democracy, and to bring their ideas to bear on the democratic revolution; to support the Chartists in England; to ally themselves with the Socialist-Democratic Party of Ledrou-Rollin and Louis Blanc in

France; and in Germany, where, under existing conditions, a proletarian revolution was still inconceivable, the Communists' task was to help the bourgeoisie to capture political power.

Marx and Engels came to Germany in 1848; shortly afterwards they dissolved the Communist League. The rightful place of the Communists was at that time held to be within the European revolution. The *"Neue Rheinische Zeitung"* (editor-in-chief Karl Marx) became the mouthpiece of ideas which were to show the bourgeoisie how to carry the revolution through and how to capture political power. Marx and Engels paid little attention to the emerging German labour movement and to the group called Workers' Brotherhood (*Arbeiterverbrüderung*) founded in August and September 1848. Faithful to their ideological interpretation of the situation, they wished to devote their efforts in the first instance to a revolutionary victory of the bourgeoisie. Only when the counter-revolution gathered strength did the paper turn also against the liberal bourgeoisie; finally it called for a "revolutionary terror" so that "the murderous death pangs of the old society and the bloody birth pangs of the new society may be cut short, simplified and concentrated". The paper now also published articles by Marx about "Wage Labour and Capital", intended to enlighten the working class. But no practical political conclusions, such as making contact with the Workers' Fraternization, were drawn.

Long after the revolution had been defeated—not only in Germany but even in the rest of Europe—Marx and Engels still did not believe that bourgeois democracy had been defeated. While Engels still fought on the side of the rebels in the Palatinate and in Baden, Marx, expelled from Germany in 1849, returned to England, where he revived the Communist League. His new watch-word was "permanent revolution", and he called on the workers to dissociate themselves from the struggle of the bourgeois democrats, to form an independent, secret and public workers' party, to arm themselves with rifles, muskets, guns and ammunition. However, he soon changed his tactics, without, however, giving up the basic idea of a democratic, proletarian revolution :

While we say to the workers : for another 15, 20 or 50 years
you have to live through civil wars and national struggles
not only in order to change existing conditions, but also in
order that you may change and become capable of holding
power—you, on the contrary, say : we must come to power
immediately or we might as well go to sleep. While we point
out, especially to the workers, how immature the German
proletariat is, you take the more popular course of outrage-
ously flattering the national consciousness and the status prejudices of the German artisan. Just as the democrats have
made the word "people" into something holy, so you have
sanctified the word "proletariat".[1]

With these words Marx upbraided those members of the
Communist League who refused to believe that the revolutionary struggle had ended and who hoped that the revolution
could be carried on permanently. The League split and, after
the Communist Trial in Cologne in 1852, was dissolved for
good. Thus Marx's and Engels' attempt to translate their
theories into political action failed in this instance and gained
them the depressing insight that ". . . in spite of everything,
the democratic, red or even communist mob will never love
us". For Marx there followed two decades of mainly proletarian existence; the fact that he and his family managed to
survive was due to Engels, who (till 1870) continued to work
in a branch of his father's business in Manchester.

In retrospect it may perhaps be said that in 1848, when
the German labour movement was founded, Marx and Engels
neglected the chance of exercising a more formative influence
upon it. The movement was initiated by *Stephan Born* (1824–
1898), a travelling printer-journeyman (later journalist and
professor in Bâle), who was a follower and disciple of Marx
and Engels. Soon after the outbreak of the revolt of the leaders
of the local workers' associations in Berlin, Born convened a
General Congress of German Workers which met on 23
August 1848 in Berlin. The congress sat till 3 September
1848 and became the foundation congress of the General
German Workers' Fraternization, the first German political

[1] From an address by Marx to the Communist League on 15
September 1849; quoted in Werner Blumenberg, "Karl Marx", Hamburg, 1962.

workers' organization. It soon had some 170 branches and district organizations, and a central committee in Leipzig, presided over by Born. It also had its own journal, "Fraternization". Fired by the possibility of active political work, Born soon found himself moving away from his mentors. He felt suddenly free of "all long term speculations", and some decades later recalled how "all communist thoughts were wiped away in one swoop; they bore no relation to what the present demanded ... What concern of mine were distant centuries, when every hour brought only pressing tasks and plenty of work."[1] We note here a conception of the emancipation of labour which was quite different from that which Marx and Engels tried to establish theoretically: the proletarian revolution and the communist society of the future are replaced by social reforms in a democratically organized state.

> The workers of Germany must strive to become a moral force in the state, a strong organism able to withstand every storm, always forging ahead, holding down and removing everything that hampers an improved state of affairs; it must accept every one whose heart is torn by the misery of the oppressed, who is himself fettered by the power of capital, whose physical and mental powers have to be at the service of the fortunate few; everyone who works or wants to work. (From the first number of "Fraternization", 3 October 1848.)

> Moreover—and it is well that our brothers, the workers, know it—we condemn rioting and we protest against every kind of disorder. We are not plotting against the existing government, we only want to be given a place in our common fatherland. ("Fraternization", 5 November 1848. Probably written by St. Born.)

Born's concrete aims were a parliamentary democracy based on universal suffrage, the right to combine, the creation of producer and consumer unions, travel grants for journeymen, labour exchanges, the organization of a progressive health service, sickness and death benefits.

Fraternity and solidarity were to enhance the ethical level of the social and political demands:

> The basis of fraternization is mutuality and solidarity. Only

[1] St. Born, *"Erinnerungen eines Achtundvierzigers"*, Leipzig, 1898.

through them can we achieve the desired end. Our watch-
word must be one for all and all for one. ("Fraternization",
20 April 1850.)

The bearers of these political ideas were the skilled workers
in small manufacturing concerns and factories, as well as the
craft apprentices and qualified factory workers. This "qualified minority among the manual workers" lacked the proletarian awareness of the class struggle in Marx's sense. Indeed
they thought of themselves as quite distinct from the proletariat of unskilled workers, navvies and day labourers, and
from the *Lumpenproletariat* which was at that time largely
regarded as a part of the criminal world. There could as yet
be no question of a distinctive class antagonism between the
bourgeoisie and the proletariat; even less of an awareness of
the necessity of revolutionary class war.

Yet in 1848, following a lengthy period of preparatory
development, there occurred a break-through towards a new
social self-awareness. Those same journeymen, master-craftsmen and skilled factory workers who had refused to be proletarians, who wished to live as burghers among burghers,
who addressed each other proudly as "Mister", now called
themselves workers and saw themselves as members of the
estate of workers, of the working class. Such social self-know-
ledge demonstrates the gulf which exists between Marx and
Engels on the one hand, and the German labour movement
of 1848 on the other. The highly insecure situation of the
journeymen who roamed abroad before 1848 had made them
susceptible to religious doctrines of salvation, and rapturous
about Communism. They were not concerned with the ultimate ends of the theory which they were being taught, nor
about whether these ends could be achieved. The German
workers of 1848 differed from these journeymen by the realistic insight into the political tasks which confronted them,
namely the implementation of their political and social
demands under given circumstances, through joint action
within a secure organization, and thus the establishment of a
new state and a new society.

The dualism of social revolution and social reform, of proletarian consciousness and bourgeois-inspired pride of status,

had its origins in 1848; it was later to be reflected in increasingly acrimonious arguments between different camps within the social-democratic labour movement. Though the failure of the 1848 revolution at first frustrated all attempts to found an independent labour movement, we can nevertheless discern both personal and organizational links which connect this period with the year 1863, when the German General Workers' Association (*Allgemeiner Deutscher Arbeiterverein*) was founded.

In 1854 the Workers' Brotherhood was banned by federal law, and only non-political and denominational workers' associations were permitted.

The parties to the conflict of 1848—Conservatives and Liberals—lacked insight into the social questions of the day; the former regarded them as a moral and religious problem, the latter as a matter of education. Both were concerned—also after 1848—with the question of how to use the political and social movements of the new estate for their own ends. Thus when, in 1848, the large landowners of Prussia founded the Union for the Protection of Property and for the Furtherance of the Welfare of All Classes of the Nation, their programme was to examine ways and means of improving the situation of the working class "in a manner which would accord with the eternal laws of human intercourse".

CHAPTER II

1850–1870

1. *The Beginnings of Industrial Expansion*

The real industrialization of Germany did not get under way till 1850 when it laid the foundations of the industrial expansion which was to make Germany into one of the leading industrial countries in the world.

The German *Zollverein* of 1833–34 introduced almost unrestricted freedom of trade and unified customs duties for goods from abroad over an area of eighteen states with a population of 23 millions. In the twenty years that followed, other German states joined the Customs Union. But Germany became a unified economic entity only after political unification culminated in the foundation of the German Reich in 1871. The building of railways and the development of other means of communication also contributed to the country's industrialization. The elimination of foreign competition (by the protective tariffs of the *Zollverein*) increased economic initiative. The favourable state of the market—albeit interrupted by crises, e.g. in 1857–59, and by famines due to bad harvests, e.g. in 1867—encouraged the growth of industry after 1850; the rate of growth of heavy industry considerably exceeded that of consumer industries both in volume and importance. Individual industries began to gravitate to certain regions. Since the manufacture of iron required coal, heavy industry developed in the Ruhr and in Upper Silesia; the textile industry, being least dependent on external conditions, remained in its old strongholds : Westphalia, Swabia, Lower Rhineland and especially in Silesia and Saxony, where the complementary industries—machine and tool manufacture— also settled. The large railway junctions—particularly Berlin, but later also Kassel and Munich—attracted the manufacture of locomotives and rolling stock.

Few reliable figures exist for the numerical growth of the working class in the two decades between 1850 and 1870. In the 'sixties most factories still employed between 30 and 100 workers (compared with 100–500 in England). It was not till after 1870 that real industrial expansion began in Germany. Wages continued to fall till the end of the 'fifties when they reached their nadir. Up till then the employers pushed the extensive exploitation of the labour force to its utmost limits; but from then on they began to exploit the labour force intensively, by refined production methods and higher hourly pay for increased output.

The varying demands made upon the workers in the production process and the comparative importance of particular industries led to the introduction of different wage rates in individual industries as early as 1850–70.

The revival of political activity among German workers from the end of the 'fifties onwards cannot, therefore, be attributed to an increase in their numbers—documentation for this is in any case lacking; it must rather be ascribed (as in 1848) to a minority of skilled workers, whose political activity was influenced by distinguished political leaders and inspired by the general political development of the day.

2. Lassalle–Marx

The German General Workers' Association was founded on 23 May 1863 in Leipzig. Its statute states its aims as follows :

> In the conviction that an adequate representation of the interests of the German working class and the abolition of the class conflict in society can only be achieved by universal, equal and direct suffrage, the signatories hereby constitute an association for the German federal states, to be called *Allgemeiner Deutscher Arbeiterverein.* Its purpose is to work by peaceful and legal means, particularly by influencing public opinion, towards the establishment of universal, equal and direct suffrage.

In these words we find the programmatic expression of the political ideas of Ferdinand Lassalle.

Ferdinand Lassalle was born in 1825 in Breslau, the son of a

Jewish merchant. Like Marx he studied in Berlin, again mainly philosophy. As a fellow member of the Communist League he met Marx in 1848. In 1849 he was sentenced to six months imprisonment on the charge of "inciting to violent resistance against state officials". From 1854 onwards he lived in Berlin, devoting himself to his philosophical writings which also formed the subject of his correspondence with Marx and Engels. In Berlin Lassalle entered public life in the interests of the workers. He devoted the last two years of his life— between the spring of 1862 and the summer of 1864—to the labour movement to the exclusion of all his other interests.

On 12 April 1862, in the Berlin suburb of Oranienburg, Lassalle addressed the machine workers of Borsig; his speech was published as the "Workers' Programme"; in July 1862 he travelled to London to persuade Marx and Engels to join him in his plans. But no agreement was reached. In the autumn of 1862, having returned to Berlin, Lassalle entered the lists against the Prussian German Progressive Party; in February 1863, following a request by the workers of Leipzig to take up their cause, he formulated the "Open Letter to the Central Committee for the Convention of a General German Workers' Congress in Leipzig"; when the German General Workers' Association was founded in May 1863, he became its president. There followed a period of ceaseless campaigning on behalf of this organization throughout Germany. In January 1864 he published his polemic against the liberal founder of a co-operative movement, Hermann Schulze-Delitzsch. Various conflicts with police and judiciary, as well as consultations with the Prussian Prime Minister, Otto von Bismarck, fall into the same period. In the summer of 1864 Lassalle went to Switzerland for a holiday; he died there as a result of a duel, on 31 August 1864.

In his analysis of the situation of the workers in a capitalist system Lassalle largely agreed with Marx and Engels, i.e. in dealing with this question he followed Marx and such "bourgeois" economists as Rodbertus and Ricardo. He spoke of classes and the domination of classes, and of the inevitable pauperization of the proletariat, which he derived from the theory of the "iron law of wages", according to which the wages of the working class can never permanently exceed the subsistence minimum. Lassalle shared Marx's grasp of the historical situation; his theoretical convictions, like those of

Marx, grew out of the argument with Hegel. Like Marx, Lassalle was aware of the dichotomy between man's freedom and predetermined development, a dilemma which was later to affect palpably the ideological self-awareness of the socialist labour movement in Germany.

> One can never make a revolution; all one can ever do is to endow a revolution which has taken place in the actual conditions of a society with the outward signs of legality, and to give consistency to its course. To want to make a revolution is the foolish idea of immature people who have no conception of the laws of history. ("Workers' Programme".)

Lassalle's interpretation of the role of the proletariat in history also resembles that of Marx and Engels :

> This fourth estate, whose heart thus contains not even a seed of a new privileged status, is for that very reason synonymous with the whole human race; its freedom is the freedom of humanity itself, its rule the rule of all. ("Workers' Programme".)

Lassalle's ideas about ultimate aims were conceived entirely on communist lines; in a letter to Rodbertus, with whom he conducted a correspondence, he says that the redemption of land and capital from private ownership represents "the innermost core" of his views. The connection with the "state Socialist" Rodbertus points to the crucial difference between Marx and Lassalle, namely their diametrically opposed views on the role of the state in the emancipation of the working class :

> Thus the purpose of the state is to bring about the positive unfolding and progressive development of man's nature, in other words, to realize the human purpose, i.e. the culture of which the human race is capable; it is the education and the development of the human race into freedom. ("Workers' Programme".)

> The task and purpose of the state consists exactly in its facilitating and mediating the great cultural progress of humanity. That is its job. That is why it exists; it has always served, and always had to serve, this very purpose ... ("Open Letter".)

Thus Lassalle seems to have hoped that, once the working classes were emancipated, the existing state would continue to fulfil this task and purpose; he was in fact convinced that human freedom, which to him was synonymous with "the cause of the fourth estate", could be realized only within the framework of the state: "It is the function of the state to bring about this development of the human race into freedom" ("Workers' Programme").

Lassalle's political programme for the labour movement sprang from these theoretical insights. He advocated the formation of an autonomous organization, independent of the bourgeoisie; representation of the working class in the German legislative bodies by means of universal, equal and direct suffrage; the establishment of state-aided producers' co-operatives to counter-balance capitalism; the appeal to the sense of equity, to reason and the will to freedom of the majority. He hoped that by such "peaceful and legal" means a just social and political order could gradually be created.

Whether Lassalle conceived the state, within which the "development of the human race into freedom" was eventually to take place, in terms of a parliamentary democracy, must remain an open question, since we lack the author's explicitly expressed views on this subject. Was it to be a parliamentary democracy or an "integral" democracy based on the "spontaneity of the popular will", on the revolutionary act of the leader, and the "dictates of science"? The manner in which Lassalle organized the German General Workers' Association seems to lend considerable support to the view that he had the latter kind of democracy in mind.

The concept of democracy remained closely linked in Lassalle's mind with that of the nation. In "the principle of free, independent nationalities" he saw "the basis and source, the mother and the root of the very concept of democracy" ("The War against Italy and the Task of Prussia"). It was, therefore, the task of the workers, who in any case had to win the struggle for democracy, to strive concurrently for national freedom. This, in the case of Germany, meant national unification.

After the end of the political conflicts which followed the failure of the 1848 revolution, from about January 1851 onwards, Karl Marx started on his analysis of capitalism in order "to uncover the economic laws of motion" of the bourgeois-capitalist society. The basic ideas of this work date back to the mid-forties. In 1851 Marx still hoped to finish his economic studies within five weeks; in the event, they occupied him during the remaining half of his life. His "Contribution to the Critique of Political Economy" was published in 1859, and the first volume of his magnum opus "Capital" appeared in 1867. The second and third volumes were published posthumously by Engels in 1885 and 1894 respectively. Between 1905 and 1910 Kautsky edited and published the "Theory of Surplus Value". A collection of the preparatory work for "Capital", carried out in 1857–58, was first published in Moscow in 1939–41 under the title "Principles of the Critique of Political Economy".

Marx's economic theory (whose essential features I shall outline in a simplified form) rests on the English economists Adam Smith and Ricardo, and the Frenchman Say, but goes far beyond them. Marx starts out from the polarization of the bourgeois-capitalist society into capitalists and proletarians, i.e. into owners of the means of production on the one hand, and the propertyless, who can only dispose of their labour on the other. In order to exist, the proletarians are forced to offer their labour as a commodity for sale in the labour market, and to sell it for a time and at a price, i.e. for a wage, to the owners of the means of production. Though the worker usually receives as much for his labour as is needed for reproduction, i.e. to restore his strength to work, the value of the goods which he creates in the production process is higher than the reward which he receives for his work. The difference between the reward of the worker and the value of the produced goods is the surplus which, after the deduction of all other cost factors, represents the capitalists' profit.

This surplus, which the capitalist is constantly seeking to increase (by increasing working hours and lowering wages, or by decreasing the working time necessary to produce goods by mechanization of the production process), is used to accumulate, i.e. to increase capital, and not primarily for consumption, i.e. private use. According to Marx, the capitalist economy is characterized by production for profit and not for consumption. The ceaseless, competitive striving of the capitalists to increase the productivity of labour by additional investment, improved production techniques, etc., leads, according to Marx, to the tendency for the profit rate to fall; smaller businesses become unable to invest increasingly large amounts, they cannot stand up to the competition of large enterprises, and are absorbed by the latter. Marx calls this process the concentration of capital.

To this concentration there corresponds the increasing size and pauperization of the proletariat: artisans, capitalists, farmers—in short the middle strata—are driven out by competition and become proletarians. But the value of labour, i.e. the price for the commodity which the worker offers, falls not only because the proletariat is growing numerically, but also because of the division of labour—made possible by mechanization—into simpler, easily learned work processes, so that unskilled, i.e. cheap, labour can replace qualified, skilled, i.e. dear, labour. The growth of the proletariat on the one hand and the displacement of the worker by the machine on the other increase unemployment, and lead to the creation of an industrial reserve-army. The competition within the labour market grows and wages fall. Thus the accumulation of capital corresponds to the accumulation of misery: "The accumulation of wealth at one pole of society involves a simultaneous accumulation of poverty, labour torment, slavery, ignorance, brutalization, and moral degradation, at the opposite pole . . ."[1]

Cyclical crises and depressions caused by overproduction are part of the inner dynamics of capitalist production and of the anarchy which it essentially resembles; they turn out to be a "specifically capitalist mechanism" (Sweezy) to refill the industrial reserve-army when periods of prosperity have so reduced it that its wages are no longer low enough to secure surplus and accumulation for the capitalist. The crises accentuate the tendency of the capitalist to capture new, uncapitalized or undercapitalized markets in other parts of the world. This, however, does not eliminate crises; on the contrary, they eventually become world-wide.

The capitalist system cannot resolve its inner contradictions.

[1] Karl Marx, "Capital", xxxiii, 4, Everyman's Library, 1930.

The prodigious growth of the productive forces in industrial capitalism will shatter the production relations (which according to Marx means the ownership relations) of the bourgeois-capitalist society (i.e. private ownership of the means of production). Thus capitalism creates the presuppositions for Socialism which will resolve the contradictions of capitalism by transferring the private ownership of the means of production into the hands of society as a whole :

> This expropriation is brought about by the operation of the immanent laws of capitalist production, by the centralization of capital. One capitalist lays a number of his fellow capitalists low. Hand-in-hand with such centralization, concomitantly with the expropriation of many capitalists by a few, the cooperative form of the labour process develops to an ever increasing degree; therewith we find a growing. tendency towards the purposive application of science to the improvement of technique; the land is more methodically cultivated; the instruments of labour tend to assume forms which are only utilizable by combined effort; the means of production are economized through being turned to account only by joint, by social labour. All the peoples of the world are enmeshed in the net of the world market, and therefore the capitalist régime tends more and more to assume an international character. While there is such a progressive diminution in the number of the capitalist magnates (who usurp and monopolize all the advantages of this transformative process), there occurs a corresponding increase in the mass of poverty, oppression, enslavement, degeneration, and exploitation; but at the same time there is a steady intensification of the wrath of the working class—a class which grows ever more numerous, and is disciplined, unified, and organized by the very mechanism of the capitalist method of production. Capitalist monopoly becomes a fetter upon the method of production which has flourished with it and under it. The centralization of the means of production and the socialization of labour reach a point where they prove incompatible with their capitalist husk. This bursts asunder. The knell of capitalist private property sounds. The expropriators are expropriated.[1]

Thus, within the very womb of capitalism the conditions

---

[1] Karl Marx, "Capital", xxiv, 6, Everyman's Library, 1930, pp. 845–6.

for the revolutionary uprising of a politically organized proletariat develop (as described in the Communist Manifesto),
and this, leading to the dictatorship of the proletariat, will
open the way to a classless society and to the withering away
of the state.

The struggle of the proletariat against the bourgeoisie will,
in the view of Marx and Engels, first be fought within
national confines, but these national struggles will then inflame
a world-wide conflict. Thus for Marx and Engels there could
on principle be no solidarity of interest of the workers and
the ruling classes within a nation. The only true solidarity is
the class solidarity of the workers of all nations against the
ruling classes of all nations. The rule of the proletariat will
ultimately abolish national differences and distinctions more
thoroughly than this has hitherto been possible under the rule
of the bourgeoisie (cf. Communist Manifesto).

Just as every society is, for Marx and Engels, a class society
in which the owners of the means of production exploit the
propertyless, so every state—including parliamentary democracy—is for them an instrument of class war. A democratic
republic is an instrument for the furtherance of capitalist
class-interests and for the oppression of the lower class, the
proletarians. Nevertheless it is of crucial importance to the
ultimate revolutionary struggle. For in no other form of state
can the last, decisive struggle between the proletariat and the
bourgeoisie be fought out (cf. Engels, "The Origin of the
Family, Private Property and the State", 1884).

Already in the Communist Manifesto we note that the dictatorship of the proletariat was considered to be by its nature
democratic and republican; this conception remained unaltered in Marx's work on the Paris Commune ("The Civil
War in France", 1871); Engels was later explicitly to confirm
that the democratic republic was "the specific form for the
dictatorship of the proletariat".

According to Marx and Engels, the last function of the
state will be to create the instruments of the political power
of the proletariat in the transition phase of the dictatorship
of the proletariat. "The state will not be abolished, it will
wither away". This idea may already be discerned in Marx's
polemic against Proudhon, "The Poverty of Philosophy"

(1847); it reappears in the Communist Manifesto, and is later discussed in detail by Engels (first in *"Anti-Dühring"*).

> We are now rapidly approaching a stage in the development of production at which the existence of these classes has not only ceased to be a necessity, but is becoming a positive hindrance to production. They will disappear as inevitably as they arose at an earlier age. Along with them the State will inevitably disappear. The society that organizes production anew on the basis of a free and equal association of the producers will put the whole State machine where it will then belong : in the museum of antiquities, side by side with the spinning wheel and the bronze axe.[1]

Only with the advent of the classless society, which Marx and Engels call "an association, in which the free development of each is the condition for the free development of all" (Communist Manifesto), can they envisage a "true democracy". As we know, they did not explicitly state what shape this true democracy would take; to have done so would have meant to indulge in what they regarded as "utopianism".

The German labour movement thus had two theories to choose from when deciding what its ends and means were to be : the social-democratic reformism of Lassalle, with its affirmation of the national state, and the international, revolutionary Socialism of Marx and Engels.

Marx and Engels took up an increasingly hostile attitude towards Lassalle, though no open break occurred; Lassalle impressed them as perhaps the only man in Germany who could take up the cudgels against the bourgeoisie.

In trying to win the support of the German worker for his aims, Lassalle met with the opposition of *Hermann Schulze-Delitzsch* (1808–1883). Schulze came from the town of Delitzsch in Saxony. Having been dismissed, in 1851, from the legal branch of the civil service because of differences with the Prussian authorities, he devoted himself to organizing master-craftsmen and tradesmen on a co-operative basis. A strict Liberal, he opposed all state intervention in the economy and regarded the co-operative as a timely self-help organization of the lower middle class against large industry. He was

[1] F. Engels, "The Origin of the Family", A Handbook of Marxism, Gollancz, 1935, p. 332.

very successful; the credit co-operatives in particular proved very effective, for they enabled small tradesmen and craftsmen, who had hitherto been excluded from all credit facilities, to work with the capital of others. Yet Schulze-Delitzsch had little understanding for the situation of the factory workers; he recommended to them essentially the same self-help measures as to the lower middle class. The workers were to change their situation by their own efforts, by thrift and solidarity, thus allying themselves economically (as well as politically) with the Liberals. Schulze-Delitzsch's transitory influence on the workers of Prussia in the decade between 1853 and 1863 was mainly due to the still strong attachment which they felt for the idea of the estates, but partly also to the fact that the workers still identified themselves fully with the political demands of the Liberals. This changed only when the German General Workers' Association was founded in 1863.

3. *The First German Labour Parties*

The "new era" in Prussia, inaugurated by the ascension of William I (who, unlike his brother and predecessor, did not wish to lean on the ultra-conservative forces) and the Italian unification movement, gave, towards the end of the 'fifties, a new impetus to the German democratic movement which had been suppressed and paralyzed since 1848. In 1859 the German National Association (*Deutscher National-verein*) was founded to provide a political organization for those Liberals who were orientated towards Prussia; in Prussia itself the liberal German Progressive Party (*Deutsche Fort-schrittspartei*) was constituted, while in Leipzig the Tradesmen's Educational Association (*Gewerblicher Bildungs-verein*) was founded. Concurrently, educational associations for factory workers and artisans developed in many German cities. A minority group in the Leipzig educational association, which pressed for independence from the Liberals and for political discussions, was the seed from which grew the German General Workers' Association (*Allgemeiner Deutscher Arbeiterverein*, ADAV). On their initiative, The Central Committee for the Convention of a General German Workers'

Congress was constituted; in October 1862 the Committee sent a workers' delegation to Berlin to discuss possible political co-operation with the National Association. Schulze-Delitzsch informed them that it was still too early for workers to be included as members of the National Association, but that they might regard themselves in the meantime as "spiritual honorary members".

In February 1863, the Central Committee requested Lassalle to draft for them an outline of a programme. On 1 March 1863 he sent them his "Open Letter", and barely three months later the ADAV was founded in Leipzig. Thus Lassalle became the leader of a small but viable party. His following among the workers' associations did not, by any means, include all of them, and the initial results of his tireless campaign were not very satisfactory: in the first year only 4,600 members joined. However, by the time he died, Lassalle had brought about the ascendancy within his party of a group which favoured centralization; the watchwords of his programme—universal franchise and associations—became firmly established among the political ideas of the workers. The leaders who followed Lassalle were less fortunate in their handling of the party's affairs, and frequently involved it in various crises. However, a start—and in the context of German politics a very sensational start—had been made: an independent German labour party was now in existence.

Lassalle's political tactics demanded that he should direct the full force of his campaign against the liberal bourgeoisie. Here was the arch-enemy who still held the majority of workers in thrall to his ideology, an enemy who had betrayed the democratic demands of 1848 which Lassalle now reiterated on behalf of the labour movement. If Lassalle was to establish an independent organization of the workers, the struggle against this arch-enemy was a pressing political necessity. He therefore feigned a tactical alliance with the Prussian monarchy (there existed, at the time, a particularly acute conflict between the Prussian Liberals and Bismarck), and quite consciously made this pretence part of his tactics. He counted on Bismarck's support in the question of suffrage, and on the help of the state for the development of producers' co-operatives. Lassalle was as correct in his view that the bourgeoisie could no longer be regarded as an ally of the workers, because it would, at crucial junctures—such as 1848—always lay down arms before the monarchy and the aristocracy, as he was mistaken in his assessment of the monarchic, authoritarian structure of the state and the society in Prussia.

If Marx and Engels thought Lassalle's demands for producer associations suspect—they already saw the workers as "pensioners of the Prussian police state"—his one-sided attack against the bourgeoisie seemed to them even worse. In their opinion, i.e. in conformity with the tactical concepts enunciated in the Communist Manifesto, the workers had to lend their support to the bourgeoisie so long as the latter fought against the reaction; under no circumstances could it be part of the workers' task to support reactionary forces. Marx and Engels also disapproved of the isolation of the working class, which was due to the workers' party being restricted to the urban, industrial proletariat; they wanted to see the rural proletariat included. A few years later they criticized the policies of Wilhelm Liebknecht, their fellow exile for many years, and of his comrade-in-arms, August Bebel, alleging that the two German politicians did not proceed with sufficient dispatch when severing their party's connection with the anti-Prussian, petit-bourgeois democracy, and had in consequence delayed the establishment of a labour party of their own. For Marx and Engels the unification of Germany, though not the leadership of Prussia, represented historical progress.

Wilhelm Liebknecht (1826–1900) came of a family of scholars and civil servants, studied theology, philosophy and philology, and in 1848–49 took part in the revolution, i.a. in the Baden rising. In 1862 he returned to Berlin from his exile in London. He had by then become a convinced follower of Marx and Engels, though he remained deeply attached to the liberal ideas of the 1848 revolution. His politics were primarily those of a man of sentiment and a pedagogue, and his significance lies not so much in the field of marxist theory and of the history of ideas as in practical politics. In 1865 he was expelled from Berlin and went to Leipzig, where he was soon to become acquainted with August Bebel.

August Bebel (1840–1913) was a master-turner who, after some years of journeying, settled in Leipzig. In 1863 he did not join Lassalle, but remained in the tradesmen's educational association, where he opposed all attempts to give the association a political character. He went so far as to oppose universal suffrage, because he held that the workers still lacked the necessary political maturity. He still fought the followers of Lassalle in the summer of 1865, accusing them of "only waiting for an opportunity to raise the banner of Communism with all its attendant horrors". His conflict with Lassalle led him to Marx, and he was on the way to becoming a Socialist when, in 1865, his meeting with Liebknecht took place in Leipzig. Both men professed the doctrines of Marx and Engels; both were opposed to Prussia and in favour of a unified Germany; and these shared convictions caused them to join in common political action.

Liebknecht's dominant political motive at that time was his opposition to the Prussian police state; hence he and Bebel accepted as their main allies the Liberals of Southern Germany whose attitude was pro-German, anti-Prussian and therefore libertarian. In this spirit and with the support of the workers' educational associations, Liebknecht and Bebel founded the Saxon People's Party (*Sächsische Volkspartei*) in 1866, after the Prussian victory over Austria. The Liberals had two reasons to be pleased with the fact that the party was so broadly based : firstly, because many of them honestly believed that the strength of democracy depends on the participation of the workers, and secondly, because they wanted to avoid the creation of an independently organized workers' movement which would threaten their own. When the breach with the Liberals (who had also organized People's Parties in other German states) finally came, it was mainly due to their unwillingness to give way on social issues; but the growing self-confidence of the workers also played a not unimportant part.

After these preparatory activities, Bebel and Liebknecht, together with several Lassalleans who had seceded from their own group, succeeded, in 1869, in establishing in Eisenach a second German workers' party, the Social Democratic Workers' Party (*Sozialdemokratische Arbeiterpartei*). The two parties did not primarily differ on political or economic issues, but diverged in their attitude to the national question : the Lassalleans favoured Prussia and a federated Germany, while the Eisenach party opposed Prussia and supported a unified Germany (though not including Austria). But neither party had set itself a political and economic programme which could be regarded as socialist and revolutionary in Marx's sense. Both strove for the democratization of the state and of society by the means offered in a bourgeois democracy, i.e. through enlightenment and by gaining a majority in parliament.

While Marx and Engels can hardly be said to have had a hand in the foundation of the two workers' parties in Germany, Marx in particular soon played a leading role in the First International—the International Working Men's Association—founded in London in 1864. Marx was a member of its General Council which, for all practical purposes, he dominated; he framed the Inaugural Address as well as the statute, drafted the resolutions and manifestos for the congresses, and finally became Secretary for Germany. In his work for the International—an organization which drew together the most diverse schools of Socialism : adherents of Fourier, Cabet, Proudhon, of the anarchist Bakunin, and finally also adherents of Marx himself—Marx showed the necessary degree of political realism. Yet it was a lack of just such realism in his assessment of men and situations that threw a shadow on his relations with the German labour movement, a shadow which remained till his death in 1883. Engels did not lose his distrust of the German labour movement till the last years before his death in 1895, when he could not but be impressed by its successes.

When Lassalle started his campaign for an independent political labour organization, the German workers were by no means ready to follow him; they were, as he found, "being towed along by the obtuse lower middle class". The new stratum of factory workers and artisans threatened by proletarization was—as we noted in the case of the youthful Bebel —at first more attracted to the workers' educational associations. The slogan of these associations was social advancement and entry into society through "education and thrift", and this greatly appealed to the workers and craft-apprentices who did not want to be proletarians.

Although the franchise was universal in the five elections for the *Reichstag* between 1867 and 1877, it was not till 1871 that the first Social Democrats gained seats in it.

The first trades which, as early as 1848 and then again in 1860, organized themselves into unions, were the printers and the cigar makers. The printers, who had comparatively high professional and educational standards and were well paid, but whose economic and social security was being attenuated by mechanization, were seeking to maintain their exclusive status by organizing themselves into unions. The cigar makers, on the other hand, enjoyed little esteem, lacked the status of guild membership and were despised as outsiders; they therefore looked for an organized corporate existence which would enable them together to win the esteem which they lacked individually. Both motives—the maintenance of the old social status and the acquisition of new social prestige —furnish a good explanation for the initial hesitation of the German worker to organize along union lines; they also explain why, once social antagonism became increasingly pronounced, he showed particular self-assertiveness in the creation of his class organization.

The initial lack of social and political consciousness of the German workers also explains to a great extent the considerable tactical caution exercized by Liebknecht and Bebel when it came to the severance of the workers' associations from the liberal Democrats—a caution which Marx and Engels criticised repeatedly and violently. The people with whom Bebel and Liebknecht had to deal were—in the words of Liebknecht himself—"not all well-trained Communists, but only communist recruits, who still have certain prejudices which must be indulged".

Karl Kautsky (1854–1938), who later called himself the popularizer of Marxism in Germany, says that up to the end of the 'seventies the doctrines of Marx and Engels were known to the leading figures of the labour movement, himself not excepted, only dimly, unsystematically, and diluted with other theories.

Lassalle was the idol of the German workers both during

his lifetime and even more after his death; their political and social outlook was determined by his ideas and aims rather than by those of Marx and Engels.

Marx's and Engels' criticism of the German labour leaders rested on an incorrect assessment of the political and social mentality of the German workers: these were not moved by the great idea of an international proletarian revolution with its attendant tasks and problems, but by the misery of their daily lives, by questions of existence and profession, and by the desire to be free of restrictions, oppression and injustice. Their common struggle was to gain these freedoms for their class.

CHAPTER III

1870–1890

1. *State, Society and Economy after 1870*

The social and political balance of power in the German Empire after 1870 rested in the hands of the Prussian aristocracy of Pomerania, the March of Brandenburg, East Prussia and Silesia, and of the upper middle class representing industry, commerce and banking. The aristocracy monopolized nearly all leading positions in the army, the bureaucracy and diplomacy: up to 1918 it held a third of the commissions in the army; in 1911 eleven of the twelve chief provincial administrators in Prussia were aristocrats; and in the diplomatic service of the Reich thirty-five of the forty plenipotentiaries were of noble birth.

The political rule of the nobility in Prussia was undisputed in spite of universal, equal and free suffrage (which, however, only applied to the elections to the Imperial parliament; the Prussian Diet was elected by a "three-class franchise", in which tax assessment determined the number of votes). Thus, for instance, the agricultural workers were generally conveyed to the polls by the landlords and for a long time had to hand over their open ballot-papers to the scrutineer—usually the landlord himself. In villages which were not under the direct influence of the landlords, teachers and the clergy saw to it that the vote went to the nobility-dominated conservative party. Civil servants, particularly the provincial administrators —frequently the younger sons of the local nobility—were explicitly enjoined to champion government policy during elections. But the social and political pre-eminence of the nobility was accompanied by its economic decline, due to the need to keep up with the living standards of the bourgeoisie, to old-fashioned farming methods and to an obsolete inheritance law (entail). In consequence, there set in, at the end of the nineteenth century, a flight of the impoverished aristocracy to the anonymity of the large cities.

The upper and lower middle classes, who were instrumental in bringing about the mighty economic expansion which changed Germany within a few decades from an agrarian state into one of the premier economic nations in the world, did not manage to transform their economic supremacy into political power and to establish a democratic, parliamentary system such as was enjoyed by other West European countries. Both classes remained bound up with the monarchic and authoritarian system of government and society which, true to German tradition, became stronger and more sharply defined after 1870–71, thanks to Bismarck's successes and his manner of government. The bourgeoisie was able to share in the political and social rule of the aristocracy only by adapting its behaviour to the example set by the nobility, and by developing an autocratic manner which corresponded to the monarchic and authoritarian pattern and extended into all spheres of life : state, society, family, and professional and public life. Such an attitude meant a renunciation of all liberal principles of freedom, but this loss was compensated by the ambition to participate in the greatness, power and prestige of the Empire; all one's desires for freedom, independence and power—renounced as regards the internal order—could be transferred to the Empire's external relations. In this way the German bourgeoisie, which had made possible the great achievements of the German economy, became the exponents of that aggressive nationalism which goaded German imperialism to ever bigger exploits.

By present-day standards the Germany of 1870 was still an agricultural country : 65 per cent of its inhabitants lived in the country or in small towns. Yet it is impossible to overlook the beginnings of that intensive industrialization which set its social and economic stamp on the period preceding the First World War. These beginnings received a decisive impetus when, after the proclamation of the Empire, the country became a single administrative unit. Another crucial factor was the annexation of Alsace-Lorraine : the textile industry nearly doubled in size, the iron-ore deposits of Lorraine became the basis of the German steel industry, the discovery of potash deposits in Alsace at the beginning of the twentieth century led (together with the deposits in Central Germany) to the establishment of the German world-wide potash monopoly.

France paid Germany more than four thousand million marks in reparations. These monies led to the setting up of a gold reserve, to an improvement in the German balance of payments and to the redemption of the national debt; this in turn led to a period during which an almost unprecedented number of companies was launched, particularly in the heavy industries and the railways: between 1870 and 1874 some 857 joint-stock companies with a capital of 3,300m Marks were founded. The consequence of the partly fraudulent company promotions were the crashes of 1873–74. They were associated with the beginning of a lengthy depression which at that time hit all industrial countries. The bankruptcies and the general slump brought about a change in the government's economic policy from free trade to tariffs, i.e. government protection of industry and agriculture at the expense of the industrial workers whose cost of living rose in consequence.

Between 1870 and 1890 the economic structure of Germany became highly industrialized. This required a large number of workers of every kind: they migrated from country to town and from the Eastern provinces of Prussia to Western Germany; they worked in mines, in heavy industry, in building, on railway and canal construction—always in the hope of improving their standard of living.

In the towns and the industrial regions the result of this immigration was a rapidly worsening housing shortage, accompanied by rising rents and food prices. While the conditions of the industrial workers improved only marginally during the boom, the workers had to bear the brunt of the slump: mass dismissals which led to long-term unemployment, falling wages and—as a consequence of all this—poverty and misery.

Quite apart from the effects of the depression of the 'seventies, the growth of industries and the internal industrial competition associated with it tended to exacerbate the social evils in industrial workshops, and led to an unscrupulous exploitation of the workers and to an absolutist rule of the entrepreneur. During the miners' strike in 1889, the great industrialist Kirdorf pithily expressed the "master in my own house" attitude common among German industrialists: "Neither king nor emperor has any say in our workshops. We alone decide." Few industrialists failed to share this view which was inspired by the *laissez-faire* ideology and by the authoritarianism of the state; few of them saw any need for comprehensive social policies. Among the minority were the catholic manufacturers Franz Brandts and Ernst Abbe, the latter a partner in the Zeiss optical works and co-founder of the Schott glass works in Jena, who created the Carl-Zeiss-Foundation through which the workers could share in the profits. Other industrialists—though no less strongly wedded to the "master in my own house" attitude—were led, partly by experience and partly by paternalism, to introduce certain internal social services: they looked after their workers by setting up wage and pension funds, by providing reasonable working conditions, building family flats, and introducing a whole series of welfare provisions, including adequate training schemes. To these industrialists belong *Alfred Krupp* (1812–1887) and *Baron Carl Ferdinand von Stumm-Halberg* (1836–1901). But in this paternalistic, authoritarian system of management even the private life of the worker came to depend on the employer; the system left little room for any kind of personal initiative and even less for political and union activity.

In 1877 Krupp made a speech to his employees in which he said: "Enjoy what is granted to you. Your work accomplished, remain in the circle of your family, with your parents, your wife and children, and think upon household matters and education. That should be your policy and you will spend many happy hours. As for the high politics of the country, do not waste your breath. Higher politics requires more time and a greater insight into conditions than are given to the workers. You are doing your duty if you elect candidates recommended to you by those whom you can trust. You will do nothing but damage if you try to interfere with the helm of the legal order. And, incidentally, to talk politics in the pub is a very expensive pastime; with the same money you can do better at home." (Quoted from Schraepler, Vol. 2, p. 90.)

Stumm, speaking to his workers in 1889 about the motives for his social policies, said : "In this way I hope to make sure, far beyond my lifetime, that you will remain deaf to the blandishments of the Social Democrats ... that is the best welfare provision I can grant you or leave in my will. Remain steadfast for all time in the old, unshakeable loyalty to our noble Emperor, remain steadfast in Christian charity and the sincere fear of God ... then you will continue to prosper as much as can be expected ...". (Quoted from Schraepler, Vol. 2, p. 93.)

The political and tactical motive behind both these speeches is obvious : defence against Socialism. This defence was usually supported by the arguments of the traditional Prussian conservative paternalism, but it sometimes assumed new forms which were better fitted to modern conditions. Among these were e.g. the creation of the Central Association of Industry (*Zentralverband der Industrie*—1875) to champion the interests of heavy industry, and the founding of the Confederation of Industrialists (*Bund der Industriellen*—1895) to defend the interests of the manufacturing and processing industries. Sometimes more direct political pressure was used, as e.g. by Stumm, one of the leaders of the Free Conservative Party in the imperial parliament, who, in the period after 1890, had great influence with William II.

The strongest and most momentous expression of the uneasiness felt by the ruling classes of the Empire about the rise of the German labour movement was the so-called Anti-Socialist Law which banned all socialist organizations. There were no objective grounds on which the practical policies of the Socialists in the Empire could give rise to fears of revolution; but in the subjective view of Bismarck and the nobility and bourgeoisie, there was no doubt about the danger threatening state and society : the Social Democrats—"a party of moral degeneration, political demoralization and social dissension" (Treitschke, *"Der Sozialismus und seine Gönner"*, 1874)—would, at a given moment, destroy the foundations of the existing order. Though the Social Democrats may have contributed to this view by their revolutionary terminology and by the aggressive wording of their publications, the underlying cause of the fear of revolution and of

the hatred of Socialism was the fact that these feelings created
a kind of negative common ground at the expense of the
workers between the Prussian nobility, intent on preserving
its lordly privileges, the economically thrusting bourgeoisie,
and the middle strata whose position was threatened by the
spread of industry.

In 1878 two men, neither of them a Social Democrat,
carried out two attempts in quick succession on the life of
William I. Bismarck used this as a pretext to proceed against
the "menacing band of robbers with whom we share our
cities" and to force the "Law against the Endeavours of the
Social Democrats which threaten the common weal" through
parliament. This law, commonly abbreviated to Anti-Socialist
Law, was in the first instance enacted for three years, but in
the event extended four times till 1890. It proscribed all
organizations

> which aim at an overthrow of the existing order of state
> and society by social-democratic, socialist or communist
> activities and ... in which social-democratic, socialist endeav-
> ours, aimed at the overthrow of the existing order of state
> and society, appear to endanger public peace and particularly
> the harmony between classes.

The law also made it possible to ban social-democratic
meetings, writings and newspapers on pain of heavy penalties.
The administration of the law was vested in the provincial
police authorities, who also had the power to expel Social
Democrats from certain localities and districts.

Simultaneously, by initiating a programme of social legislation, Bismarck tried to wean the workers from the political
influence of the Social Democrats, and to win their allegiance
for the existing state. His actions were determined by tactical
reasons and possibly by some remaining vestige of practical
Christianity. Both motives were in the tradition of the social-
conservative ideas which had been advocated by an—admittedly small—number of Prussian Conservatives since the 1848
revolution. The National Health Insurance Act became law
in 1883, followed by the Accident Insurance Act in 1884 and
by the Old Age and Disablement Insurance Act in 1889.
But Bismarck refused to extend protective labour legislation.

Yet since the social legislation was parallelled by the rigorously enforced Anti-Socialist Law, it completely failed to achieve the effect which Bismarck intended. Nevertheless, it was the first social legislation in the world and as such an epoch-making, viable and genuine contribution to the social security of the workers.

2. The Social Democrats under Bismarck

Since 1869 the German labour movement was split into two organizations : the German General Workers' Association founded by Lassalle, and the Social Democratic Workers' Party led by Bebel and Liebknecht. Political differences were not confined to those between the two organizations, but existed also within the parties themselves. This became particularly evident when, at the outbreak of the Franco-Prussian war, deputies had to vote on the issue of war credits : in the North German Parliament the "Eisenachers" Bebel and Liebknecht abstained, but the "Eisenacher" Fritzsche voted in favour as did J. B. von Schweitzer, deputy of the Lassalle party whose pro-national attitude was a matter of policy. Bebel and Liebknecht justified their abstention on the grounds that "as opponents on principle of every dynastic conflict, as Social-Republicans, and as members of the International Working Men's Association" they could "neither directly nor indirectly" support the war. But the official inner circle of the "Eisenachers", the "Brunswick Committee", was of the opinion that even the Socialists "as Germans guarantee Germany". When, after the fall of Napoleon III, the war against the French Republic continued, the Eisenachers—and later also the Lassalleans—protested against the continuation of the conflict and against the planned German annexation of Alsace-Lorraine; unlike the Lassalleans, they also opposed Bismarck's slogan of "Blood and Iron", which two elements were to weld Germany together.

This opposition was not rooted in revolutionary, marxist ideas and did not represent a decision between pacifist internationalism and the nationalism of a powerful state. For Bebel and Liebknecht a vote in favour of war credits would have been tantamount to a vote of confidence for "Prussian separatism and militarism", for the "arch-enemy" of freedom and of the libertarian unification of Germany. They too were striving for a united Germany, but by means of the democratic precepts of 1848 rather than by "blood and iron"; they wanted to achieve "unity through freedom" and not "freedom through unity". The Lassalleans, on the other hand, had long ago acknowledged Prussia's claim to leadership, as Lassalle himself had done. There is no doubt that the differences of opinion about the unification of Germany, which divided the two groups, were more than a mere question of tactics; yet they did not affect the real core of the emancipation movement of German labour. On the issue of workers' emancipation agreement was so general that in 1875 in Gotha the two groups were able to merge without any drastic re-orientation on the part of either of them. The persecution and pressure by the new German state contributed to their unification. In the elections for the Imperial Parliament which followed in 1877, the new German Socialist Workers' Party (*Sozialistische Arbeiterpartei Deutschlands*) secured more than half a million votes and thirteen seats. Now, not only battalions of workers were on the march—as Lassalle had once hoped—but, as a national-liberal paper wrote at the time, "regiments, brigades, divisions, nay more, entire army corps".

The Social Democrats may have regarded themselves as "enemies of the Empire"; they may have described the German Empire as the epitome of class rule and been convinced that "not a single penny should be voted" (Bebel) for this undemocratic and anti-social system; yet they did not oppose the state as such. Neither Liebknecht nor Bebel (though the latter was eventually to modify his views) shared Marx's and Engels' ideas about the withering away of the state, but considered its function in the same light as did Lassalle and his followers; they agreed that "the purpose of the state is to bring about the positive unfolding and progressive development of man" (Lassalle: "Workers' Programme"). The attitude of the Social Democrats to internationalism was similar. There was no lack of conviction that only an internationally united working class can successfully fight against the capitalist society; but there existed an equally strong awareness of the obligations of world citizenship, obligations to the ideas of enlightenment, humanism and the French revolution, and of the fraternal links between the German and the international working class. These feelings testify to the extent to which the German Social Democrats were part of the liberal-democratic German tradition: an internationalism which rested on such foundations allowed for the claims of national obligations.

The Gotha Programme of 1875 states that, among other things, the Socialist Workers' Party

> ... fights by every lawful means for a Free State and a Socialist Society; it fights to annul the wage system and its iron laws, to remove exploitation in every form and to abolish all social and political inequality.[1]

The Social Democrats wanted to achieve their aims—a free, popular state and a socialist society—"by all the available legal means"; according to the Gotha Programme these included universal suffrage and "state-aided socialist producers' co-operatives under the democratic control of the working people". Did this mean that they renounced revolution? Leading Social Democrats had always drawn attention to the possibility that a revolution could be prevented by reforms. Did this mean that they under-estimated the class character of the state? In fact they remained, at the same time, convinced that the inevitable sharpening of the class contradictions must necessarily lead to revolution. Nor did the Social Democrats openly advocate a democratic republic; but what then was the meaning of demands which could in fact only be realized in a democratic republic? Marx, with his innate shrewdness, recognized these inconsistencies when he harshly criticized the Gotha Programme:

> Since we have not the courage—and wisely since the circumstances demand caution—to demand a democratic republic as the French labour programmes under Louis Philippe and Louis Napoleon did—we also should not take refuge in the neither "honourable" nor "worthy" subterfuge of demanding things which only have meaning in a democratic republic, from a state, which is nothing else—though embellished with

[1] Appendix IV, Karl Marx: "Critique of the Gotha Programme", Lawrence, London, 1933, p. 117.

a parliamentary form of government and intermingled with feudal relics—than a police-guarded military despotism, bureaucratically constructed and already influenced by the bourgeoisie and moreover declare into the bargain to this state that we fondly imagine we shall be able to extort the same from it by "legal means".[1]

These contradictions cannot be resolved; at best, we may try to explain them. (i) The tension between the certainty of a predetermined course of historical development towards revolution and the will to revolutionary activity and to intervention in the historical process was a concept which Marx explained by means of "the dialectical unity of theory and practice"; however, in the political thought of the German Social Democrats this concept lost its sophistication and became a mere contradiction. (ii) The concept of revolution assumed two different meanings : firstly, revolution as a spontaneous illegal uprising (which could be prevented by reforms), and, secondly, revolution based on a majority decision of the people and thus carried out within the bounds of democratic legality. Only the latter entered into the theoretical considerations of the German Social Democrats. Such a legal revolution might in certain circumstances be nothing but a consistent policy of reform. (iii) No explicit indication was given about the methods by which the goal of the workers' emancipation was to be achieved. The practical policy of the Social Democrats in the new German Empire was, unlike most of their theoretical utterances, reformist. These inconsistencies became even more pronounced by the acceptance of the theories of Marx and Engels at the time of the Anti-Socialist Law.

The Anti-Socialist Law followed on years of police oppression and persecution; thus, e.g. Bebel and Liebknecht were implicated, in 1872, in a treason trial and sentenced to two years confinement in a fortress. As a result of the Anti-Socialist Law the organizations of the party were disbanded, nearly all its papers banned, and an estimated number of 1,500 persons sentenced to terms of imprisonment and hard labour. 900 persons were expelled, and many people were forced to emigrate. The practical policies of the party remained within

[1] Ibid., pp. 46–7.

the bounds of legality (which no one actually denied—the activities of the anarchists were an exception). Even the erasure of the word "legal" from the Gotha Programme at the Party Congress held in 1880 in Wyden in Switzerland, was not basically inconsistent with this policy; it was merely meant to express the party's willingness to carry on its work even under conditions of enforced illegality. The first illegally distributed broadsheet, printed in 1878, contained the following appeal to members :

> Do not let yourself be provoked ! ... Resist all attempts to lure you into secret societies or insurrection ! Hold fast to the watchword which we have so often repeated to you : Our enemies must perish at the hands of our legality.

This remained the unshakable resolve of the party leadership. And when, in 1890, the Imperial Parliament did not extend the Anti-Socialist Law, these tactics were held to have been fully justified by events, so that Wilhelm Liebknecht was able to say : "In the long run, brute force must yield to moral factors, to the logic of events". After a temporary setback, the number of votes cast for the party also continued to increase, and this in spite of the Anti-Socialist Law :

1871 124,000 (3·3 per cent); 1874 352,000 (6 per cent); 1877 493,000 (9·1 per cent); 1878 437,000 (7·5 per cent); 1881 312,000 (6·1 per cent); 1884 550,000 (9·7 per cent); 1887 763,000 (7·1 per cent); 1890 1,427,000 (19·7 per cent).

The Anti-Socialist Law depicted the workers as "fellows without a country" and thus as outside the German state whose establishment they had, ever since 1848, desired at least as fervently as had the bourgeoisie. Only now—as Bebel himself admitted—did the disappointment with the state, whose fundamental role in the emancipation of the workers had been stressed since the days of Lassalle, culminate in a hostility, full of bitterness and hatred directed against the state. Only now did the doctrines of Marx and Engels gain among the German workers the ascendancy which Marx had wrongly assumed to have existed in 1875, when he said of the party leaders who supported the Gotha Programme that they "were committing a terrible outrage against the generally accepted opinions of the mass of the party".

Apart from the work of *Eduard Bernstein* (1850–1932), who edited, first in Switzerland and then in London, the party's paper *"Der Sozialdemokrat"*, the spread of marxist theories was mainly due to Karl Kautsky, founder of the journal *"Neue Zeit"* (1883). But we must not overestimate the extent to which the German workers accepted the doctrines of Marx and Engels. They had become acquainted with the Communist Manifesto and the first volume of "Capital", whose ideas they had usually acquired through the many popularizations (particularly those of Karl Kautsky). But an analytical understanding of Marxism was not essential to them; what they needed, in order to survive as outcasts from their own nation, and what they believed to have found in Marx, was the certainty of a necessary collapse of the bourgeois society and the victory of Socialism.

Their enforced isolation confirmed the party leaders and their followers in the conviction that the labour movement had no allies, that the emancipation of the workers was the exclusive task of the working class. A radical ideology, cleansed of all the remains of liberal, bourgeois views, transformed their intolerable isolation into a confident solitude which looked outward, towards a secure future. The aggressive phraseology of Marx and Engels, which so impressively reflected their revolutionary radicalism, closely matched the bitterness and indignation felt by the workers under the Anti-Socialist Law. The need for a radical ideology grew in spite, or rather because, of the law-abiding policies of the party. But if Marx and Engels were beginning to modify their distrust of the German labour movement, they were mistaken in their premisses: for even under the Anti-Socialist Law the German Social Democrats did not become a revolutionary, power-seeking party, but remained one of the "normal, professional parties of European workers" (Rosenberg, *"Demokratie und Sozialismus"*).

The professional character of the workers' party and the associated tendency to reformist policies left their mark on the work of the party, particularly when, at the time of the Anti-Socialist Law, this was virtually confined to parliamentary activity. The leadership of the party fell to the parliamentary group; parliamentary action, backed by growing electoral successes, appeared more and more to be the right way to power. This tendency did not remain uncontested, and led to conflicts even during the period of repression. In the 'nineties it led to the establishment of a radical Left wing. Thus even at the time of the Anti-Socialist Law there existed, objectively, a discrepancy between the radicalism of theory and the reformism of practice: but this divergence had no subjective existence.

CHAPTER IV

1890–1914

1. *Social Conditions and the Social Self-Awareness of the Workers before 1914*

The "golden era of world economy"—those three decades before the outbreak of the First World War—was for Germany a period of further uninterrupted economic development, characterized by the formation of monopolies and cartels. Thus, e.g. the Rhenish-Westphalian syndicate controlled nearly 100 per cent of the (hard) coal production in the Rhineland and Westphalia; the electrical industry was dominated by two giant concerns, AEG and Siemens; in 1910 nearly 50 per cent of all bank deposits were distributed among the five major Berlin banks: the German Bank, the Discount Company, and the Dresden, Darmstadt and Schaffhausen Banking Unions. The process of amalgamation of the big banks started before the First World War, while their ties with industrial concerns grew apace, so that soon every major bank was closely connected with one of the leading industrial groups.

The mighty industrial expansion is also made evident by the fact that the number of workers doubled between 1887 and 1914; the percentage of unemployed remained steady at just over 2 per cent. There was an increasing tendency towards shorter working hours, and real wages rose more rapidly than in other industrial countries (between 1885 and 1910 by 100 per cent). And while average wages rose by 37·5 per cent between 1895 and 1907, the cost of living increased by only 22·5 per cent. In this context we must also mention the achievements of the workers' insurance institutions: around 1900 they covered five and a half million persons, to whom 5,000 million marks (in 1912 10,000 million) was paid out.

The accession of Emperor William II inaugurated another era of social legislation in Germany, directed mainly towards the protection of the workers and the provision of certain legal safeguards. In 1891 the relevant portions of the existing statute, the Imperial Industrial Act, were replaced by a newly drafted Workers' Protection Act : this included regulations to prevent danger to life and health, ordinances relating to the length of the working day (no industrial work on Sundays, a maximum 11-hour day for females, a ten-hour day for young persons; neither females nor young persons to be employed on night shifts), the banning of child labour under thirteen in industrial occupations, and a section about the possible establishment of workers' committees in places of work. Further statutory provisions relating to the protection of children, young persons and women were enacted in 1900 (being amendments of the relevant sections of the Imperial Industrial Act), followed in 1903 by the Children's Protection Act; further legislation followed the International Convention in Bern in 1908. Industrial tribunals to settle disputes between workers and employers had been established as early as 1890; the German Civil Code, which came into force in 1900, provided the legal basis for all work contracts. After the turn of the century, a series of social and legal instruments was enacted for the protection of the new class of non-manual employees; thus in 1900 a supplement to the Industrial Act included regulations about closing hours, rest periods and accident prevention. This was followed by the Commercial Arbitration Act of 1904 and the Salaried Employees' Insurance Act of 1911.

But if we wish to gain a sober and realistic understanding of the economic and social position of the German worker before 1914, we must remember that, under prevailing food prices and rents, the average annual income of 800–900 marks would only just allow him—if his family was not too numerous—to live without pressing worries as to whether he could feed them. His family was seldom in a position where its members could at the same time afford to eat their fill, live in salubrious conditions, and be adequately clothed. Harsh economic necessity drove his wife to work either in a factory or at home, particularly if his family was large. Housing conditions provide a particularly dark chapter in this era: in 1895 Berlin still had some 25,000 one-room apartments, each housing six or more persons; these apartments were mostly in houses which stood at the back of the main buildings, away from the street, sunless and dark in the shadow of overhanging walls. At the same time there were in Berlin some 80,000 "sleeping lodgers", i.e. mostly young, single, male and female workers, who slept in a bed or part of a bed in someone else's household, and had no right of access during the day. Family life—in the sense in which this word is understood among the bourgeoisie and in the country— was out of the question; in North Berlin, as in other large cities, every third house boasted an inn, where in the evening and on Sundays the "sleeping lodgers", with nowhere to go during the day, and the fathers of noisy, overcrowded families, went to drown their sorrows in drink.

Most German workers had little to hope for before 1914; for themselves they hardly dared to hope for anything, yet all the more did they pin their hopes on their children. Not only were the workers oppressed by material cares, which were by no means a thing of the past; they were also bitterly resentful both of the way in which, in their daily work, they were dependent on "those up there"—the employer, the capitalist, the boss—and of the physical and spiritual conditions which condemned them to their lowly social position, a bondage which they considered unalterable. Their desires, therefore, always tended to centre around the same things: higher wages, further education, independence, a small house in its own grounds, an apartment—or better still—a smallholding with a few acres and an orchard, a small farm of one's own, freedom to exercise their craft and skill.

Most workers were well aware of the great gulf between their aspirations and reality; thus the visions of the future which affected them most powerfully were those which were bound up with the fortunes of their class, with the hopes for a victory of the Social Democratic Party and the creation of the state of the future. It was only when they acquired classconsciousness and the conviction that solidarity with those who shared their fate was both meaningful and necessary, that they collectively gained the self-confidence which they so often lacked individually : "We workers . . . are the pioneers of the new era!" The precepts, still very much alive, of the traditions of the peasant and artisan estates were frequently incorporated into this proletarian consciousness, which gave the ethos of the proletarian estate a certain quaintness.

The workers' resignation and hopelessness were only relieved by the advent of the collective social class-consciousness which made bearable the deep abyss between the workers and the members of other classes, and provided an outlet for the universally frustrated energy of the individual.

> I believe in social revolution by way of evolution. I am by nature an optimist and I do not hope—I know. Whether I will be better off financially, I cannot tell. But that is not important. The modern labour movement enchants me and all my friends by its ever brighter beam of knowledge. We realize that we are no longer the anvil, but rather the hammer forging the future of our children. This feeling is worth more than riches. (Lewenstein, *"Die Arbeiterfrage"*; a survey published in 1912.)

The man, who had the confidence to say : "I do not hope —I know", was a 33-year-old miner with a weekly income of 21 marks and eight children. He exemplifies the political, and indeed the psychological, significance which the doctrines of Marx and Engels must have had for the politically aware worker. But it must be admitted that the need for a rational understanding of issues, the search for concrete, tangible and "irrefutable" truths led many a semi-educated worker to narrow rationalism and futile dogmatism.

The German worker found in the labour movement a sterling substitute for the social and political status which was denied him in the Empire; the feeling of belonging to the working class, and the belief in international Socialism alone made his fate bearable. Thus the constant growth of the labour movement up to the war was not a sign of increasing radicalism, but an expression of the universally held conviction that "We, the workers, belong to social democracy".

Before 1914 the German workers were filled by the unshakable conviction that the economic development would one day sweep away the ruling class, including the Hohenzollern monarchy. If they were at all sceptical, it was about the classless state of the future, for they could not imagine a non-authoritarian state. They did not think of a revolution in terms of a violent uprising; they believed instead in a "social revolution through evolution".

Later it became even less conceivable that they should lightly risk their laboriously won achievements; all the more since the "bigwigs", i.e. the gentlemen of the imperial government, administration, army and economy, convinced that the Social Democrats would one day violently overthrow the existing order, were always inclined to provoke the labour movement into rash actions. The workers hoped to achieve their aims by peaceful means.

2. The Practical Political Activity of the Trade Unions and the SPD after the Repeal of the Anti-Socialist Law

The creation of workers' political organizations in the 'sixties gave a fresh impetus to their professional organizations, i.e. to the trade unions. In September 1869, on the initiative of the leaders of the Lassallean Workers' Associations, a General Congress of the German Workers was convened in Berlin, and the General Union of German Workers formed. Lassalle was opposed to the creation of trade unions, because his exclusive aim was a purely political movement; for this reason the Lassallean unions were in fact intended to be no more than a section of the political labour organization. Differences about form—central, local or professional—and about content—subordination to the political organization or independence in representing the interests of the workers—led to fragmentation, and finally, in 1874, under the weight of the government's repressive measures, to the complete dissolution of these unions.

In 1868, on the initiative of the German Progressive Party, the Hirsch-Duncker trade associations were created as a counterweight to the Lassallean unions; they were intended to work along liberal lines and by liberal means within the capitalist economic and social order towards an improvement of the social conditions of the working class.

The workers' educational associations, led by Bebel, and the Eisenach Social Democratic Workers' Party—after it had joined the International Working Men's Association, which, at its Geneva Congress of 1866, had declared that "the furtherance and formation of trade unions was the chief task of the working class, both at the present time and in the immediate future"—also tried to promote unions. The "International Unions", founded on the initiative of the Eisenachers, differed from the Lassallean unions by their independence from the political organization and by their decentralized structure.

In the 'seventies unsuccessful attempts were made to form centrally affiliated union organizations according to trades, and to make them politically independent. The Anti-Socialist Law, which came into operation on 21 October 1878, also affected the unions, with the exception of the Hirsch-Duncker associations, whose members had to sign an undertaking that they were neither members nor supporters of the Social Democratic Workers' Party (1876).

Trade unions gradually revived, though, being illegal, disguised, e.g. as sickness-benefit clubs; in 1890, the year of the repeal of the Anti-Socialist Law, 300,000 workers are believed to have been organized in unions; but the unions were without any kind of influence and lacked a clear conception of their task. However, as early as November 1890 we see the creation of the General Committee of German Trade Unions under the chairmanship of *Karl Legien* (1861–1920); this committee represents the first common alignment of the socialist-orientated trade unions, later to be called "free" unions to distinguish them from the christian labour organizations.

The tasks which the Free Unions set themselves were clearly demarcated from those of the Workers' Party :

> The difference between the political activity carried on by the Workers' Party and the tasks of the unions rests on the fact that the former seeks to transform the organization of existing society, while the efforts of the latter, being circumscribed by law, are anchored in present-day bourgeois society. (Appeal to Union members, 1891.)

The unions wanted to fight to improve the pay and working conditions of the workers within the framework of bourgeois society; their weapon was to be the solidarity of its members. This work appeared to them to be a means to an end—the transformation of the economic, social and political power structure—rather than an end in itself. It would succeed only if the power and size of the trade union organizations were equal to those of the employers. For this reason their watch-word from the very beginning was: "The power of the unions lies in their organization" (Legien, 1898). But they also understood the need for comprehensive educational activity and the significance of the unions as "cultural factors of the highest importance".

The Free (and later the Christian) Unions were organized centrally, according to trades, and affiliated to the main General Committee (after 1919 the General Confederation of German Trade Unions—*Allgemeiner Deutscher Gewerkschaftsbund, ADGB*); the local unions were organized along the same lines under local cartels. This manner of organizing unions was not considered acceptable in all instances, and, for a long time, existed side by side with independent unions, individual trade associations with a professional bias, and local groups whose interests were political rather than trade-unionist. Numerically insignificant, the latter tended towards syndicalism, which was widespread in the Latin countries, and advocated self-help by "direct action" in preference to parliamentary and trade-union methods. The process of amalgamation and centralization of the Free Trade Unions continued till the First World War; more than 60 per cent of their members were organized in the six major trade unions, those of building-, metal-, manufacturing-, wood-, textile- and transport-workers, while the rest of the membership was spread over forty-one other unions. As the unions gradually penetrated into large concerns, so the principle of organization by industry (i.e. a single union for all workers in a certain industry regardless of their trade) slowly gathered momentum.

Membership figures for the Free Trade Unions amounted to 237,000 in 1892, 680,000 in 1900, 1·8 million in 1908 and 2·6 million in 1912. In 1907 trade-union funds amounted to 33 million marks, compared with 1·3 million of the SPD.

The trade unions tried to provide comprehensive social support for their members: during strikes members received strike pay; the victims of lock-outs and other countermeasures

by the employers received victimization pay; dislocation payments and removal contributions were available to those who
had to move to obtain work. So as to exert an influence on
the labour market, the unions set up labour exchanges. Local
secretariats looked after the legal interests of members.

The main area of union activity was the fight for higher
wages and salaries, and for the reduction of working hours.
Between 1885 and 1910 unions achieved an increase in real
incomes of nearly 100 per cent for their members, but were
unable to bring about an eight-hour working day till the
November Revolution of 1918. Though the number of strikes
and lock-outs up to the First World War was very high and
almost constantly increasing, the number of successful wage
agreements without strikes grew apace. Throughout, the
unions were intent to conclude wage agreements which would
have the widest possible application. In 1913 almost 13,500
rates-of-pay agreements were reported, covering some 218,000
concerns with over 2 million workers.

The unions also energetically promoted the social rights of
the workers. Union representatives acted as assessors in
industrial and trade courts, as members of arbitration tribunals
dealing with social insurance; they represented their fellows in
chambers of commerce, in the labour exchanges, and collaborated with factory inspectors in the elimination of social
grievances.

The growing importance of the trade unions as a decisive
factor both within the labour movement and in the economic
and social framework of the state generally is reflected in the
growing number of union leaders in the SPD group in the
Imperial Parliament: in 1893 their share of seats was only
11·6 per cent, but by 1912 this had risen to 32·7 per cent.
Their parliamentary activity was not confined to collaboration on issues of social legislation or to the fight against
economic policies which adversely affected the standard of
living of the workers (as, e.g. the custom tariffs of 1902), but
extended to general political issues, e.g. the Prussian "three-
class" franchise. In these questions the union leaders' attitudes
often diverged from those of the party leaders (as we shall
see in some detail later).

The unions had strong personal and financial ties with the

co-operative movement. It was not till 1903 that the socialist-orientated co-operative societies split from the producers and trade co-operatives created by Schulze-Delitzsch, and became, with the support of the Free Trade Unions, the Central Association of German Consumer Co-operatives (*Zentralverband deutscher Konsumvereine*). The importance of the consumer co-operatives as part of the self-help of the German worker is best shown by the sober statistics of the Annual Report of the Central Association for 1911 : according to it, there were 1,142 local co-operatives with 1·3 million members and a turn-over of 335 million marks.

After the repeal of the Anti-Socialist Law, the Social Democratic Party grew into a mass movement covering the whole German Empire. This can be seen from the membership figures and the electoral successes after 1890 :

(*a*) The following membership figures are available for the period after 1906 (in thousands) :

1906 384; 1907 530; 1908 587; 1909 633; 1910 720; 1911 836; 1912 970; 1913 982; 1914 1,085.

(*b*) Election year	Seats	Votes cast in millions	Proportion of votes in per cent
1890	35	1,427	19·7
1893	44	1,787	23·3
1898	56	2,107	27·2
1903	81	3,011	31·7
1907	43	3,259	29·0
1912	110	4,250	34·8

Policy and tactics were laid down at the annual party congress which was attended by delegates of the individual constituencies (their number being determined by the membership figures). Even on minor points the delegates were frequently mandated by their constituency parties. The party congress issued directives to the parliamentary group and expected from it, as also from the executive committee, an account of their activities. The executive was elected annually; in practice it was almost invariably re-elected. The executive transacted the business of the party and constituted, together with the control committee, the party leadership. The parliamentary party maintained, even after 1890, the strong position it had acquired during the period of the Anti-Socialist Law, though this was not formally acknowledged. As the differences of opinion about the ends and means of the labour movement grew inside the party, so the importance of regional party organizations—which, on certain highly controversial issues (e.g. the budget appropriation vote), did not follow the party line—also increased.

The work of the parliamentary group was hampered by the party's fundamental opposition to both the internal and the external policies of the state. The parliamentarians tried to look after the interests of their supporters by loyally co-operating in legislation; but their consistent refusal to pass the budget appropriations of the Empire amounted to a permanent abdication of the power to which their numbers, based on the will of the electorate, entitled them. Not till the general elections of 1912 did the Social Democrats try to break through this political inertia which was dictated by purely theoretical considerations: by making an official electoral agreement in respect of the Second Ballot with the Progressive People's Party, they entered, for the purpose of achieving their political aims in Parliament, into their first alliance with other democratic forces. In 1913 the parliamentary group, now the strongest single party, used its political power in the interest of its voters in the debate about new taxation which was to pay for increased military expenditure. In the period before 1914 the SPD never managed to arrive at a clear decision about the best way to employ its constantly increasing political and organizational power and about whether and how to exploit its parliamentary strength. The party was torn between the fear that a policy of compromise would dilute its basic principles and lead to the neglect of the all-important struggle against the class-state, and, on the other hand, the need to use every means to achieve the final goal by splitting the forces of its opponents and gradually assuming leadership.

However, in the Land parliaments, in the majority of which the SPD was represented since the turn of the century (in 1903 by a total of 101, in 1912 by a total of 231 deputies), the party succeeded at an early stage in exploiting conflicts between the other parties and working towards pro-

gressive social and cultural policies. The party was also able
to make its influence felt in the drafting of new electoral laws
in Bavaria, Württemberg and Baden. In keeping with this
policy, the South German parliamentary groups voted—
against the wishes of the national party—on the budget appropriations (first in Hesse and Baden in 1891), and concluded
electoral agreements with the Left Liberal parties. After 1898
the party took part in the Land elections in Prussia, mainly to
demonstrate the injustice of the "three-class" franchise; in
1903 the SPD with 18·79 per cent of the votes cast was
unable to win a single seat, while the Conservatives with
19·39 per cent won 143 out of the possible 443 seats. Even
more impressive—by comparison with the relative inflexibility
of the national parliamentary group—were the achievements
of the SPD in the municipalities where councils furnished a
long overdue outlet for the social and welfare activities of the
women organized in the Social Democratic Party.

> In 1913 there were nearly 11,000 Social Democrats on munici-
> pal and district councils, 320 on municipal and local boards.
> During 1910 an estimated 100,000 Social Democrats worked
> in the agencies and the administration of the workers' insur-
> ance institutions, in trade and industrial courts, and in the
> municipal labour exchanges.

There is thus good reason for regarding the socialist labour
movement on the eve of the First World War as a "legitimate
component of the German Empire". The Social Democrats
and the trade unions had achieved great advances in the
social, political and cultural emancipation of the German
worker within the framework of the existing monarchic and
authoritarian order; they had succeeded in establishing the
labour movement as a factor which had to be taken into
account in a state and society they had once set out to fight.
Yet the degree to which the workers were integrated in, and
could identify themselves with, the existing system remained
restricted. It is true that there were many opportunities,
particularly in the field of social policies, for collaboration
even with government departments (who finally even sent
representatives to the union congresses), and that with every
passing year a growing number of employers, regarding the
unions as partners in industry, entered into wage agreements

with them; yet the attitude of the ruling classes continued to be determined by an aggressive rejection of the labour movement—be it socialist or not—whom they regarded as a serious threat to their established positions of leadership, and against whom, right up to the First World War, they entered into coalitions, whose constituent groups had no other interest in common.

> Thus in 1894 the labour movement was threatened by the so-called Subversion Bill, which proposed to deprive the Socialists of their right to vote; in 1899 by the so-called Convicts Bill, which proposed heavy penalties for strikers who interfered with those willing to work; in 1904 a National Association against Social Democracy was founded in Berlin and continued to operate till the outbreak of war.

The Social Democrats and the trade unions could, therefore, succeed in furthering the emancipation of the workers against the opposition of the ruling class only by organizing labour in such a way as to provide external protection against the often extreme aggressiveness of their opponents and a measure of internal security in essential spheres of life. German labour was thus relegated to a ghetto-like existence, albeit in a positive sense of the word.

> From 1900 women became increasingly active in the SPD; the Socialist Labour League of Youth began to spread in 1904; in 1906 a Central Education Committee was set up to plan and direct the educational work of the party; in 1906 the Party School was started in Berlin for the training of the party's officials. At the same time workers' sports clubs and other leisure organizations multiplied. The Workers' Teetotaller Association also assumed some importance. More controversial, however, was the Association of Freethinkers, founded in 1905, which later became the Central Association of Proletarian Freethinkers.

3. Programme and Aims of the Social-Democratic Labour Organizations between 1890 and 1914

In 1891 the German Social Democrats, whose party now bore the name of Social Democratic Party of Germany (*Sozialdemokratische Partei Deutschlands*—SPD), adopted a new programme at Erfurt. The introductory part, concerned with principles, had for the most part been drafted by Kautsky; it adhered dogmatically to the doctrines of Marx and Engels, particularly to those of the "Capital", and stressed, in its very first sentence, the "natural necessity" of economic development of the bourgeois society towards the socialization of the means of production. The practical part, drafted by Bernstein, contained demands whose premisses acknowledged the existing state as a basis for the improvement of the social and economic condition of the workers, e.g. demands for universal and equal suffrage (i.a. in Prussia), for equal rights for women, for the secularization of schools, comprehensive labour legislation, and freedom of association. This obvious programmatic dualism could—from the point of view of Marx's theories—be resolved through the "dialectic unity of theory and practice" which relates reformatory work and revolutionary goals. (Marx himself had demonstrated this by his work in the First International.) Interpreted in the light of this conception, the programme seemed to contain no inconsistencies.

But as Marx and Engels had never given an unambiguous interpretation of the relation between the economic determinism of their philosophy of history on the one hand and their ethically motivated political activism on the other, it was possible that under certain political and psychological conditions the concept of a "dialectical unity of theory and practice", of predetermined revolution and free human action, would fall apart; if this were to happen then Kautsky's interpretation with its stress on the determinist and evolutionary element of Marx's theories would tend to gain ascendancy. According to Kautsky, the Social Democrats were a "revolutionary, but not a revolution-making party".

> ... and since the revolution cannot be arbitrarily staged, we cannot make the least pronouncement about when and under which conditions it will occur. (K. Kautsky "*Sozialdemokratischer Katechismus*", Neue Zeit, 1893.)

After the repeal of the Anti-Socialist Law, the majority among the German Social Democrats were convinced "that the development of our present capitalist society will by itself reach such an acute stage ... as to make it necessarily grow into a socialist society". These words were spoken in 1891 by Karl Grillenberger, a Bavarian deputy. In their rejection of "street fighting, barricades and such like uprisings" (Bebel) the Social Democrats thought of themselves as following Engels, who, shortly before his death, in March 1896, wrote in his preface to a new edition of Marx's "Class Struggles in France 1848–1850" that "... the spell of the barricade is broken, street fighting belongs to the past". He considered the conditions for the modern class struggle to have changed, particularly as a result of the German workers' successful use of universal suffrage; this seemed to him "an entirely new method of proletarian struggle".

> And so it happened that the bourgeoisie and the government came to be much more afraid of the legal than of the illegal action of the workers' party, of the results of elections than of those of rebellion ...

> The irony of world history turns everything upside down. We, the "revolutionaries", the "rebels"—we are thriving far better on legal methods than on illegal methods and revolt.[1]

For Engels this only meant that, following the experience of the Anti-Socialist Law, the tactics for achieving the final, revolutionary goal had changed, and that legal means were to be used till it became possible to make the leap from legal agitation to revolutionary action; he did not renounce revolutionary methods in principle. While Engels believed himself to be in accord with the German workers' party, whom he considered actively revolutionary, they, in their turn, called on him as on their chief witness to confirm the correctness of their self-analysis, according to which they were "revolutionary, but not revolution-making".

Had the German Socialists consistently adhered to this analysis, then they should have taken no action to improve the social and economic conditions of the workers; for reforms inhibited the class struggle and retarded the "necessary" course of events leading to the collapse of capitalist economy and society. The task of the party should then not have gone

[1] From: "A Handbook of Marxism", Victor Gollancz, London, 1935, pp. 85, 92.

beyond electoral propaganda and the organization of the masses to prepare them for the revolution which would come but could not be arbitrarily brought about. The success or failure of elections would then have been the barometer indicating the state of the proletarian movement and the supposed degree of approximation to the final revolutionary goal.

But for a party which relied on the masses the restriction to such a spurious revolutionary inertia would have represented an internal inconsistency; and it was for this reason that the Right wing of the parliamentary party regarded Bebel—who, at the Party Congress of 1903, described himself as "the mortal enemy of bourgeois society"—as a die-hard revisionist. Here we see the significance of Kautsky's interpretation of the party's revolutionary theory · it concealed the rift between political action and ideological claims, and provided the semantic means for reconciling the reformist practice of the party with the revolutionary aims of international Socialism. This emerges quite clearly from Kautsky's conception of the nature of the revolutionary :

> However, everyone is a revolutionary who strives towards the seizure of power by a hitherto oppressed class. He does not lose this character by wishing to prepare and accelerate the capture of power by social reforms which he tries to wrest from the ruling class. What distinguishes a social reformer from a social revolutionary is not that he seeks to bring about social reforms, but that he explicitly confines himself to these reforms alone. (*"Die soziale Revolution"*, 1902.)

The political practice of the German Social Democrats, which we described earlier, prompts the question why no one should have tried to superimpose a suitable theory on their reformist practical work (as Bernstein demanded), why no one "explored towards the Right, when the way to the Left was closed, or was believed to be closed" (Max Weber's criticism); why, in fact, the theory of international, revolutionary, proletarian Socialism was not abandoned. The German labour movement remained a minority movement till 1914—discriminated against in the German Empire and denied both social and political equality. The consciousness that capitalism and the rule of the class-state were doomed to collapse, and the awareness of unity and common purpose with the international working class gave the German workers a collective confidence which could not have developed on the stony ground of their homeland. If we look at this situation from the point of view of group psychology, we come to understand the attraction, exercised on the German worker, of the idea of ultimately achieving a classless, rulerless society, the utopia of the "promised land" of the future socialist state. In his "Woman and Socialism" Bebel gave the classical exposition of this future society; the book sold hundreds of thousands of copies.

The revolutionary theory had the further function of unambiguously differentiating the Social Democrats from the bourgeoisie; for those same workers who, on a personal level, cherished petit-bourgeois dreams, would have found it intolerable if their party, the party of the international proletariat, had been no more than one party among many. Moreover, the revolutionary theory as advocated by Bebel and Kausky offered a common denominator which drew together all schools of thought, so that the social and political unity of the labour movement could be maintained; and this unity was the premiss for the successful accomplishment of the historical task of workers' emancipation.

The revolutionary theory in its Kautskyan interpretation (sometimes called "Kautskyism") was thus an attempt to put an ideological cover on the psychological and political stresses engendered by the German workers' pariah-like position in the German Empire. Such an attempt may well have been vitally important for the survival of the socialist labour movement; yet we cannot overlook the fact that the dogmatic adherence to the revolutionary theory hampered the political leadership of the German workers' party when it came to the framing and the execution of a programme of political action which would lead to the seizure of power.

Jean Jaurès, the French socialist leader assassinated in 1914, speaking about this issue at the Amsterdam Congress of the International in 1904, said:

> Behind the rigidity of your theoretical formulations which Kautsky will produce for you to the end of his days, you conceal from your own and from the international proletariat that you are incapable of action.

In 1907 another disillusioned French Socialist, Gustave Hervé, said of the German Socialists that they "are by now no more than election and counting machines of a party with mandates and insurances"; "you want", he said, "to conquer the world with ballot papers". (Stuttgart Congress of the International, 1907.)

Such a description of the German labour movement, though perhaps exaggerated, was by no means false. According to the official revolutionary ideology of the party, its task was to prepare the proletariat for the class struggle, to intensify its activity and effectiveness, and to increase the party's power by demonstrations and canvassing at election time. Nothing was said about how the party was to use its constantly growing political and organizational power. Since, according to Kautsky, the revolution could not be arbitrarily brought about, and since nothing could be said about when and under what conditions it would occur, no ideas existed about the concrete way to power : organization became a substitute for political action.

It was obviously believed that one day the SPD would gain an absolute majority in parliament, after which it would either assume power more or less without a struggle, or— and this seemed more probable—the ruling classes would resort to unconstitutional methods and stage a coup. The latter eventuality would force the workers to use all available means of combat, including, as Bebel emphasized, mass strikes. This belief paid no regard to the fact that, by insisting that the party confine its propaganda to industrial workers only, a limit was set to the spread of its influence. Admittedly, the party successfully extended its canvass to the catholic industrial workers and to the agricultural labourers East of the Elbe, and attracted a certain number of fellow-travellers from the lower middle-classes and the countryside who were dissatisfied with conditions in the Empire; it also exercised a certain attraction on intellectuals. Many Jews joined as well, because only within the labour movement could they expect the recognition and realization of their political and social emancipation. But the party's efforts lacked the necessary intensity for any outstanding successes to be achieved, all the more since it could hardly be expected that the lower middle-class and the farmers would join the very party which predicted the decline and proletarization of the middle strata through economic development.

The Lassallean thesis that—apart from the workers—all sections of the population are "only one reactionary mass" (cf. the Gotha Programme) lingered on; Marx and Engels had vigorously opposed it (especially Marx in his "Critique of the Gotha Programme"); they saw not only the need to collaborate with other Left liberal parties in certain situations, but also the necessity of opening the ranks of the party to the middle strata; only thus could the German workers' party remain both the "only genuinely progressive party" and at the same time "the only party strong enough to enforce its progressive demands" (Engels, 1895). In reality the SPD was an isolated party of one class, the class of the German industrial workers. The sharp distinction between "social-democratic" and "bourgeois" persisted till just before the First World War; this was partly due to the pariah-like position forced upon the Social Democrats in the Empire, but partly also to their own inflexible attitude engendered by official party ideology. The belief in an economically predetermined revolution and the blind adherence to Marx's refusal to furnish "recipes for the cook-shop of the future" provided a welcome psychological justification for the lack of political activism and for the absence of any concrete ideas about the use of the party's constantly growing power. Arthur Rosenberg's description of this attitude may have been rather exaggerated, but it is not altogether unfair :

> In general, the Social Democratic Party official had no real interest in problems of foreign policy and the army, education, the administration of justice, the civil administration, and even agrarian problems. He never realized that the day might come when the Social Democrat would be called upon to decide all these matters. His interest was concentrated solely upon everything that concerned the technical interests of the industrial working class in the narrow sense of the term. In this sphere he was both well informed and active. Outside it he was perhaps interested above all else in the suffrage question.[1]

[1] Arthur Rosenberg, "A History of the German Republic", London, 1936, p. 13.

The unrevolutionary mentality of the party's members was another obstacle to a consistent exploitation of the strong political position which the party had gradually acquired; they were not equal to the challenge of revolutionary activity against the existing state and social order. Had the leaders of the party asked the masses to engage in a revolutionary political struggle and risk once more all the gains already achieved, they would have found themselves isolated from the rank and file. Nor were the party and trade-union officials, who had achieved a secure social status through the labour movement, ready to endanger the work and functions upon which their new status rested. These features reinforced the German labour movement's tendency towards inflexibility. This was further strengthened by an element of conservatism which was implicit in the tasks which the unions now had to perform in a state and society enjoying a long period of stability : the workers had to be protected against exploitation by the ruling class, and social and political achievements had to be safeguarded and extended.

The leaders of the labour movement were convinced that the ruling class would not surrender its leading position without a struggle and that it would respond to any kind of revolutionary endeavour by destroying the labour movement. However much this idea may have been justified, it also showed the extent to which the party underestimated its own powerful position. No wonder that critical contemporary observers did not regard the members of the German socialist labour movement as revolutionaries, but rather as "good, contented and well fed Philistines" (Hervé) of "thoroughly middle-class deportment", with "the faces of comfortable publicans" (Max Weber). Even if this generalization is not altogether fair, there is no doubt that the petit-bourgeois deportment of the party's members reflected their political and social mentality : they were attached to their organization and willing to make sacrifices for it, intent on personal advancement and education, hopeful that things would improve for their children, and radically opposed to the prevalent "Prussianism".

The efforts of the party's leadership to explain the far-reaching social and political activities of the workers' organizations in terms of formal, ideological radicalism did not remain unchallenged. In 1891 the leader of the Bavarian Social Democrats, *Georg von Vollmar* (1850–1922), made two speeches in Munich in which he outlined a reformist programme in keeping with Southern German opinion :

> In a word : we have our principles, but their application to life, the political tactics, depend on the political and economic conditions and needs prevailing at any one time, and are largely determined by the conduct of those in power and by the other parties (Mommsen, p. 334).

Vollmar and the Reformists (as distinct from the Revisionists), particularly the party's secretary *Ignaz Auer* (1846–1907) and the Chairman of the General Committee of the Free Trade Unions, Karl Legien, refused to enter into theoretical discussions and speculations about the future, and instead sought—as Vollmar said—"to bring about economic and political improvements in the interest of the labour movement and of the community in general, on the basis of the present order of state and society".

Thus, e.g. Vollmar was able to collaborate in the drafting of the Erfurt Programme; at party congresses most Reformists voted for resolutions put forward by the Centre, represented by Bebel and Kautsky, particularly if these were directed against the Revisionists. They were not in principle uninterested in theoretical questions, but did not wish to have their practical policies trammelled by the exigencies of a new theoretical system; they may also have been convinced that the party could fulfil its function of integrating all workers only if it maintained its ideologically-based claim of being the revolutionary party of the international proletariat. Thus the Reformist Auer could chide the Revisionist Bernstein : "My dear Ede, the sort of thing you ask for is not done by passing a resolution; one does not say it, one does it".

Because of their power, the trade union leaders occupied a special position among the Reformists. After 1900 the conflicts about the independence of the trade unions within the labour movement created a rift even among the Reformists, particularly after both Ignaz Auer, representing the party executive, and Bebel defended the exclusive right of the party to determine the political guiding lines for all workers' organ-

izations. Such claims were an expression of the organizational
patriotism of the party and rested on arguments which clearly
derived from the ideas of Lassalle, Marx and Engels about
trade unions. Lassalle's attitude may be described as only a
little short of anti-trade unionism : his exclusive interest
centred on the workers' political organization for the class
struggle. Marx and Engels, on the other hand, clearly understood the possible—though admittedly limited—effectiveness
of the unions. The unions could improve the economic position
of the worker within the capitalist system; they could also
help to bring about the final, revolutionary stage of the class
struggle by eliminating mutual competition among the
workers and making them aware of their power against
capitalism. But for Marx and Engels this form of struggle was
never an end in itself; it was always subordinated to the "goal
of seizing political power".

The trade unions, whose numbers, financial resources and
activities in the field of social policy were in any case superior
to those of the party, finally won their point. The SPD Congress of 1906 declared that the importance of the trade unions
was equal to that of the party; and the executive committees
of the two bodies received a directive to the effect that "in
order that concerted action may be taken in cases which
concern equally the interests of the trade unions and the
party, the central leadership of the two organizations should
try to reach an agreement". The trade unions never contested
the right of the party to formulate the theoretical basis of
the political aims and the future plans.

The disagreements about the independence of the trade
unions were closely linked with the question about the conditions under which mass strikes should be used as means of
political struggle. The debate about political mass strikes was
set off by the impact of the Russian revolution of 1905, and
by the successes of the Swedish and Belgian Socialists, who
used a general strike to achieve universal suffrage. Should
not political mass strikes also be used in Germany to combat
the Prussian "three-class" franchise and the erosion of the
franchise in Saxony? The most consistent advocate of political
strike action was Rosa Luxemburg. Yet whenever the question
of political strike action, of downing tools or of staging May

Day demonstrations arose, the leaders of the trade unions were always concerned that nothing should be done to jeopardize the existence of their organization and their gains in the field of social policy.

Undoubtedly the effectiveness of the trade unions against the employers lay in their cohesion and in the invulnerability of their organization. It must also be remembered that up to the First World War the trade unions largely relied on workers in craft industries and medium sized concerns (i.e. on skilled workers), and that their influence only gradually spread to major concerns (with their large numbers of unskilled workers). The unions had to be particularly circumspect when it came to organizing labour in large-scale industries where the employers (unlike the workers) were themselves well organized.

As a result of this one-sided emphasis on the struggle for improved working conditions, the trade unions—like the party—found themselves completely unprepared for the tasks which the new, democratic structure of the post-1918 economy imposed on them.

A general strike, i.e. the highest form of revolutionary mass strike, was rejected as strictly inadmissible in the German context not only by the trade union leaders, but by Bebel, Kautsky and Bernstein; instead, they favoured political mass strikes by individual trades or regions, regarding such strikes as the ultimate weapon to be used only in extreme situation, e.g. under the threat of disenfranchisement or if the right to organize was threatened.

It need not really surprise us that Eduard Bernstein, the spokesman of the Revisionists, agreed with this view—though admittedly not without qualifications. The "gradual growth into Socialism" which he postulated could only be achieved under democratic conditions. His attempt to bridge the gulf between the party's theory and its practice was intended to revise not the practical policies of the party, but rather the theory which was at odds with them. He wanted the party to give up its obsolete phraseology, so that its image would match what had for a long time been its real character, namely that of a democratic, socialist party of reform. Bernstein believed that his endeavours conformed to Marx's and Engel's economic theory of history which he wanted to

apply to newly observed facts so as to give a new impetus to
the policy of his party and provide it with a body of theoretically secure tactical concepts.

"I set myself against the notion that we have to expect shortly
a collapse of the bourgeois economy, and that social democracy should be induced by the prospect of such an imminent,
great, social catastrophe to adapt its tactics to that assumption . . . (So Eduard Bernstein wrote in a letter to the Social
Democratic Party in October 1898).

Instead of speculating about the great economic crash, so
he argued, it was the task of Social Democracy "to organize
the working classes politically and develop them as a democracy and to fight for all reforms in the State which are
adapted to raise the working classes and transform the State in
the direction of democracy".[1]

The Left and Centre of the party bitterly attacked Bernstein's revisionism and he was outfought at the Party Congress
of 1903, though his ideas continued to influence a section of
the party. Considered in retrospect, Bernstein may well have
been right to demand a revision of the theory on the grounds
that new insights about the dynamics of the bourgeois-capitalist economy and society contradicted Marx's predictions
in some respects (e.g. the impending collapse of capitalism).
Indeed, he may have been a better disciple of Marx than his
opponents. Yet, like Lassalle before him, he overestimated
the chances of the Social Democrats to bring about structural
social and political changes with the limited means of pseudo-
parliamentarianism at their disposal. This erroneous assessment was partly based on the mistaken hope that the "Left
wing" of the bourgeoisie would become politically active in
the interest of democracy. Bernstein also underestimated the
importance which the traditional, radical theory, as interpreted by Kautsky, had for the collective self-confidence of
the German workers.

The radical Left on the other hand—whose main protagonists were *Rosa Luxemburg* (1870–1919) and *Karl Liebknecht* (1871–1919)—believed that the only way to achieve
a socialist social order was by means of the "hammer blow

[1] Eduard Bernstein, "Evolutionary Socialism: a criticism and
affirmation" (Preface), The Socialist Library, 7, London, 1909.

of the revolution", which they imagined as "a result of the tenacious and unremitting revolutionary struggle of a large class-conscious popular mass".

> The seizure of power by the proletariat, *i.e.* by the great mass of people, cannot be brought about artificially. It presupposes ... a certain degree of maturity of the economico-political conditions ...

> Only in the course of the political crisis which accompanies the seizure of power, only under the fire of long stubborn struggles, can the proletariat achieve the necessary degree of maturity ... which will make it capable of the final great upheaval. (Rosa Luxemburg, *"Sozialreform oder Revolution"*, 1899.)

Rosa Luxemburg thus accepted work for practical reforms as a tool for the revolutionary education of the proletariat. Later, however, under the impact of the Russian revolution of 1905 and in consequence of the growing self-identification of the Social Democrats with the existing state, the radical Left came to regard political mass strikes and insurrection as the crucial revolutionary weapons in the struggle of the German labour movement. In formulating its political tactics, the radical Left disregarded the real attitude of the allegedly revolutionary masses. Yet common political action might have resolved the ideological disagreements within the party : on the Left there was at least some limited acknowledgement of the importance of practical reforms; and on the Right, Ludwig Frank, one of the most liberal minded Reformists, gave thought to the "total mobilization of the party's resources to serve the democratization of Germany". Victor Adler, the leader of the Austrian Socialists, also saw the chance of uniting the party by common political action; in 1903, on the eve of the Party Congress in Dresden, he wrote to Bebel :

> If you were to indicate ... the broad lines of a programme of action, and say that this and this are the points at which we have to push with all the might of our three millions, if you were not—unlike K.K. (i.e. Karl Kautsky)—to appeal to the programme which, by saying everything, says nothing, then you would carry the whole party congress with you ... (Adler, *"Briefwechsel"*, pp. 422–3)

CHAPTER V

1914–1918

1. *Toward a National State*

"The working men have no country", says the Communist Manifesto of 1848. Indeed, the generation of socialist workers, whose formative years coincided with the Anti-Socialist Law, had the feeling of being excluded from the nation, of having no part in its life. But the effect of school, military service, and of the monarchic, authoritarian order of state and society generally, not only gradually modified this feeling, but brought about a "process of nationalization" which few Socialists consciously acknowledged. For many of them it was no more than simple pride of the German worker's world-famous efficiency and skill which seemed to them to surpass those of workers in other countries; initially, it may have been no more than the traces left by a constant confrontation with the values of a military tradition and the ideas of a nationalistic state. These values and ideas—devotion to the cause of the fatherland, subordination to national greatness—turned many a fellow without a country into a well-disciplined "wearer of the Emperor's colours", who would later, at work or over a pint, enthusiastically proclaim : "We are both soldiers and Social Democrats, body and soul". Added to these sentiments was the justified pride in the hard-won social and political achievements which the labour movement had gained by its own exertions. The workers themselves had created values which appeared to them worth defending against internal as well as potential external enemies. They were no longer the proletarians who had nothing to lose but their chains.

This applied not only to the rank and file; the proponents of the official policy of the Social Democrats also seemed increasingly impressed by the arguments of the national, power-centred state which asserted that Germany could not support its working population without constantly creating new markets, that world-wide expansion was needed, which in turn pre-supposed Germany's supremacy in Europe and a powerful fleet. In 1913 a large majority of the SPD deputies voted in favour of the new tax laws which were to provide additional monies for military expenditure. They thus abandoned the principle of "not a man, not a penny for this system", which they had upheld for several decades. Yet, in spite of this relatively far-reaching acceptance of nationalist, power-orientated ideas, the SPD remained alive to the dangers of the ill-conceived foreign policy of the Empire and often drew attention to its probable consequences.

The unqualified advocacy of the defence of the fatherland had a long tradition which was in no way inconsistent with the views of Marx and Engels. They had not contested the right to independence and self-defence, though they expected that every war would be used to advance the interests of the international proletariat. There is no doubt that allegiance to the national traditions of 1848 found expression in the views of Marx and Engels, just as it most certainly influenced the thinking of Bebel and, even more profoundly, that of Liebknecht. In 1870 the leaders of the Eisenachers made it known that in the Franco-Prussian conflict "they were ready resolutely to defend the integrity of German soil against the arbitrary action of Napoleon or anyone else". Even while the Anti-Socialist Law was still in force, Auer, Liebknecht, Bebel and others repeatedly stated that their party was ready "to render the same duties to the fatherland as did all other citizens" (Auer); in summer 1913, a few weeks before his death, Bebel, speaking in a debate on army estimates, said :

> There is not a single person in Germany who would surrender the fatherland to an enemy without a fight. This is particularly true of the Social Democrats . . .

Though such pronouncements were meant to refer solely to the defence of the state in case of an attack by other powers, there were some Social Democrats who were quite ready to acknowledge the value and importance of the national state as a matter of principle, with all the political consequences which flowed from such an attitude. In 1907, at the Congress of the Socialist International at Stuttgart, Vollmar proclaimed that

> ... it is not true that international equals anti-national. It is not true that we have no fatherland. My love of humanity cannot prevent me for a single moment from being a good German, just as it cannot prevent others from being good Frenchmen or Italians. However much we recognize the common cultural interests of nations, however much we fight against and condemn their being incited against each other, we cannot conceive the utopian idea that nations should cease to be and coalesce into an amorphous porridge of peoples.

These statements must be considered against a background of disagreements within the Second International about international anti-militaristic actions and the use of the general strike as a political weapon, particularly to avert a war. The majority of the socialist parties, with the Germans and Austrians in the lead, rejected the idea of a general strike in wartime, since they did not believe that the Social Democrats in any country were strong enough successfully to rise against the power of the state at the outbreak of hostilities. Concerning anti-militaristic actions in peace time, the German Socialists in particular, according to their spokesman Bebel, were determined not to let themselves be hustled into using methods "which might be fatal to the party's affairs, possibly to its very existence" (1907, Stuttgart). This attitude was partly due to the conviction that the ruling class in Germany would not stand idly by while the political power of the Socialists increased, but would resort to force. It was contended that no pretext must be given to provoke such intervention; not only so as to avoid endangering the very organizations upon whom the power of the labour movement rested, but also in order to preserve the German worker's social progress which it had taken half a century to achieve.

The Socialists in France—who were no less strong than those in Germany (1914, 1·4 million votes and 103 seats in the Chamber of Deputies)—and in Britain thought differently : they advocated political mass strikes as a method to oppose war. Their views were undoubtedly partly determined by the fact that the socialist parties in the parliamentary democracies carried more weight and exercised a greater influence in public affairs. (The French Government included a socialist Minister, Millerand, as early as 1899.) The crucial issue, in the eyes of the International, was an agreement between the German and the French socialist parties; not only were they the two major parties in Europe, but the relations between their two countries were particularly strained and traditionally antagonistic. A resolution was eventually passed at Stuttgart in 1907 (re-affirmed in Copenhagen in 1910 and again at Bâle in 1912), which promised everything and nothing : it put the Socialists under the obligation "to do everything, by whatever means seem to them most effective, to prevent an outbreak of war"; but it admitted at the same time that the means adopted would in each case have to depend on the intensification of the class struggle and the general political situation. No binding declaration was issued about the kind of means envisaged, or about the possibility of sanctions by the International or its Bureau. On the contrary : the German Socialists (in particular) were determined that the International should recognize the right to national self-defence against enemy attack. Bebel was especially vocal in arguing for a point of view which the German Socialists had never abandoned :

> "If Russia, that bulwark of savagery and barbarism, that enemy of all human culture, were to attack Germany in order to dismember and destroy her—then we are as much, and indeed more, concerned than are those who lead Germany, and we shall oppose it." Russia's victory would mean "our defeat as Social Democrats". (Bebel at the Party Congress at Erfurt, 1891; "Proceedings", p. 285.)

The idea that Germany must defend European culture against Czarism might have had some factual justification before the Russo-Japanese war of 1904 and the Russian revolution of 1905, i.e. before the Czarist regime showed itself to be a colossus with feet of clay. But instinctive fear of the "Czarist spectre" remained an element of the still hidden German social-democratic patriotism which only occasionally broke surface, as e.g. when a German trade union leader (Leimpeters of the Miners' and Foundry Workers' Union) spoke at the Trade Union Congress at Cologne in 1905 against a resolution passed by the Amsterdam Congress of the International which had declared the First of May a day of rest :

> Where will this lead? In the end the English, the Hottentots, and the Chinese will tell us at the International Congresses what we, in Germany, are to do.

From 1907 onwards, the high moral and political esteem enjoyed by the German Socialists in the International began to wane; the importance of the International declined. Before long the great European socialist parties also took the road towards their own national states; compared with their German brethren, the obstacles in their way were fewer. In their eyes, Prussian Germany, with whom the German Socialists seemed increasingly to identify themselves, assumed the role which the German Socialists had hitherto reserved for Czarist Russia.

The degree to which the German Socialists identified themselves with the existing national state was necessarily incomplete : Prussian Germany remained a class-state under authoritarian rule, even though international Socialism was gradually losing its lustre. In an effort to fill this vacuum, the social-democratic consciousness acquired a very peculiar accretion, namely a kind of social-democratic sense of mission. The mission was to preserve the values which had shaped German culture—and indeed those which were fundamental to Prussianism—to save them from falling into abeyance by giving them genuine content and reality in the face of the very people who were supposed to represent them. In other words, to achieve what the Prussian nobility and the German bourgeoisie failed to achieve throughout their history. The idea was well expressed by Bebel :

> If we really have to defend our fatherland, then we shall defend it because it is our fatherland, the soil on which we live, whose language we speak, whose customs are our own; because we want to transform this, our fatherland into a country which has no equal in perfection and beauty' anywhere on earth. (Party Congress in Essen, 1907; "Proceedings", p. 255.)

There is no other state like Prussia, and when, one day, we

shall have her in our power, then we shall have everything...
In the South they do not understand this haughty state in all
its beauty. (Party Congress at Magdeburg, 1910; "Proceedings", p. 250.)

Here we clearly discern the thread of continuity which runs
from "Emperor Bebel" (as he was nicknamed at International
Congresses), through "King Ebert", the first President of the
first German Republic, to the "Red Czar of Prussia", Otto
Braun, Prussian Prime Minister, 1920–32. The recognition of
German interests in relation to those of other countries represented a kind of detour in the thinking of the SPD: it led,
shortly before the outbreak of the First World War, to a
change in the party's attitude to the monarchic and authoritarian state; the state now appeared as "worthy" of correc-
tion, as worth the effort to make it more democratic in conformity with the tenets of the SPD. However, before this
re-orientation had any political effect, the First World War
broke out.

2. The Fourth of August and its Consequences

At the meeting of the Imperial Parliament on 4 August
1914, the Social Democrats voted unanimously for the war
credits; a dissenting minority of 14 deputies, which included
Karl Liebknecht and Hugo Haase, one of the two party
chairmen, submitted to party discipline. The parliamentary
party explained its action on the grounds that the war was
a war of defence against Russian despotism, whose victory
would present a terrible threat to the culture and independence of Germany: "We are now doing what we have always
emphatically maintained: we are not forsaking the fatherland
in its hour of peril". The SPD, like all other parties, pledged
itself to desist from all public disputes with other political
parties, and not to oppose the government for the duration
of the hostilities. The trade unions and the employers' associations had already agreed on 2 August to suspend all labour
disputes for the duration.

The attitude of the workers' organizations echoed the mood
of their supporters, for the workers, in common with everyone
else, had entered into the spirit of national elation engendered

by the outbreak of war: it seemed to them that their long efforts towards identifying themselves with their country could now at last be realized. A complete self-identification with the state swept away their feelings of isolation, insecure confidence, resignation, passivity, and the burden of their divided loyalties—to the national state on the one hand, and to international Socialism on the other.

They justified their emotional devotion to the fatherland by the conviction that in fighting Czarism they were fighting for survival; of the many proclamations and explanations published in the social-democratic press during those first August days, not a single one mentioned the fact that this fight would also involve Britain and France. These two countries, heirs to successful democratic revolutions, were instinctively liked as much as Czarism was detested. The socialist parties in France and Britain acted in the same way as the German Social Democrats; their patriotism and national consciousness were, however, bound up with the traditions of the successful democratic revolutions in their countries, whose values they now wished to defend against the autocracy of the German Empire.

The hitherto dormant nationalism of the German Socialists was also being justified on the curious grounds that it was entirely consistent with the doctrines of Marx and Engels, and with the ideas of the International. While it might just have been possible to reconcile the vote for war credits—as long as these were destined for purely defensive purposes—with the ideas of Marx and Engels, such a reconciliation could certainly not be claimed for the political truce, since, according to Marx and Engels, wars should be used to further the interests of the proletariat. Nor could a marxist conception of a democratic, parliamentary system of state and society have found room for a situation in which the SPD, having reached a position of crucial importance, desisted from all attempts to impose its will on the Imperial Government and from every effort to take a hand in the conduct of the war.

The pressure of events seemed to resolve in a radical way the disagreements which had persisted within the party for many years, though the resulting pattern did not altogether conform to that of the pre-1914 factions.

The extreme Right wing of the party, which soon came to represent the ideas of nationalism and the supremacy of the state, was grouped around the journal *"Die Glocke"* (The Bell), edited by the former radical Russian revolutionary Alexander Helphand, who wrote under the pseudonym "Parvus". This group regarded the world war as the great world revolution with Germany representing the revolutionary, and Britain the reactionary, forces. Thus a German victory was not only in the interests of the German people and the German workers, but coincided with "the future interests of international Socialism". After Germany's victory, the nations of Central Europe would be drawn together into a powerful bloc under German leadership and carry out an aggressive expansion both East and West. The home policies which corresponded to this foreign policy showed signs of incipient social Fascism : the group advocated the establishment of "organizational Socialism of a specifically German character" in opposition to the West European, liberal and marxist tradition of international Socialism.

Another group centred around the *"Sozialistische Monatshefte"* (Socialist Monthly), formerly the mouth-piece of the Revisionists; it included Max Cohen-Reuss, Max Schippel, and August Müller. The group held the comparatively moderate view that the nations of continental Europe would have to combine under the leadership of Germany to counteract the economic supremacy of the English speaking democracies.

The Left wing of the SPD eventually split into two camps. The pre-war radical Left, led by Rosa Luxemburg, Karl Liebknecht, Clara Zetkin and Franz Mehring, remained a minority; its members regarded the granting of war credits as a sign of submission to the ruling class and as the death of the International. In their view every war fought in an age of imperialism, regardless of whether it ended with Germany's victory or her defeat, was equally damaging to the interests of the working class. Their slogan was "Down with War" and their aim the revolutionary seizure of power by the working class. The first step towards this goal was to vote against further war credits. Rosa Luxemburg, writing under the pen-name 'Junius', formulated their programme in a pamphlet entitled "The Crisis of Social Democracy" (*"Die Krise der Sozialdemokratie"*, written in 1915, published in 1916). On 4 August 1914 Karl Liebknecht had bowed to party discipline, but after December 1914 he voted against war credits in Parliament; in January 1916 he resigned from the parliamentary party. A few days earlier, on 1 January 1916, a group of dissident Social Democrats, who were in sympathy with Rosa Luxemburg and Karl Liebknecht, had formed themselves into the *Gruppe Internationale*; their journal was called "Spartacus", a name which was later applied to the group itself.

After 1915 the majority group of the Left wing included representatives of the Centre of the party (Kautsky), of the moderate radical Left (Haase, Hilferding), and Revisionists (Bernstein, Eisner), all of whom shared common pacifist and democratic principles. While they did not deny the need for defensive action, they felt that the war aims and the expansionist policy of the ruling groups in the German state and society militated against the credibility of a defensive war. After December 1915 they therefore consistently voted against war credits and advocated a "negotiated peace". Nor did they subscribe to the political truce of August 1914; while rejecting direct revolutionary action such as the Spartacists advocated, they demanded more political freedom of action for the party. After being expelled from the parliamentary party in March 1916, eighteen Left-wing deputies formed their own parliamentary group. This was followed by a split among the organizations outside parliament. In January 1917 the SPD expelled the opposition, and at the beginning of April 1917 the German Independent Social Democratic Party (*Unabhängige Sozialdemokratische Partei Deutschlands*—USPD) was formed. The strongholds of the new party were in Berlin, Leipzig, Frankfurt a.M., Brunswick, Halle and Erfurt. The Spartacus group also joined the new party.

The party leadership (Ebert, Scheidemann, David), who had the largest following and were therefore called the Majority Socialists, stood half way between the Right and the Left wings of the party. In this group, a tendency existed towards coming to terms with the monarchy and the army and achieving a national democracy. Some leaders had good relations with the government and the army (Scheidemann,

David, Südekum, Max Cohen-Reuss). In the field of foreign policy the Majority Socialists in parliament dissociated themselves from policies of expansion through conquest, though some of them were not altogether opposed (e.g. David, Noske) to German economic expansion in the East, and to a Poland which—though possibly independent in other respects—would to a certain degree depend on Germany politically and militarily. In internal politics the party remained a captive of the political truce concluded in August 1914; year after year it voted unconditionally in favour of war credits, though at the same time protesting against a policy of conquest, and pressing the government to change its policies at home, more particularly to abolish the "three-class" franchise in Prussia.

Though the leadership of the Majority Socialists continued —in public and in private—to harbour certain reservations against the war policies of 4 August 1914, the leaders of the trade unions remained firmly wedded to the principles enunciated on that day. Early in 1916 the *"Correspondenz-blatt"*, published by the General Committee of the trade unions, wrote :

> The policy of 4 August accords with the most vital interests of the trade unions; it keeps all foreign invasion at bay, it protects us against the dismemberment of the German lands, against the destruction of flourishing branches of the German economy, and against an adverse outcome of the war, which would saddle us with reparations for decades to come...

Wilhelm Jansson, a member of the General Committee, held views about foreign policy which corresponded to those of the extreme Right wing of the Majority Socialists; and the General Committee's chairman, Karl Legien, insisted that in any conflict with the opposition in the party, the views of the majority must be unreservedly enforced all along the line. The measure of opportunism in the interest of the workers, to which the trade unions confessed even before war broke out, enabled their leaders, in spite of wartime restrictions, not only to prevent any erosion of the advantages gained in the past, but even to win new ground. Thus, e.g. their collaboration on legislation for voluntary service, and their co-operation

with the military in industrial concerns vital to the war effort
led to their official recognition as representatives of the
workers (in 1918 three trade unionists were included in the
semi-parliamentary government of Prince Max von Baden);
they were able to take steps towards equality with employers'
associations, and were given complete freedom to organize.
The policies of the trade union leaders had their critics among
members, particularly among the metal workers and in some
of the smaller unions. Not a few officials from the lower ranks
of the unions and from the shop floor were in sympathy with
the USPD. Eventually workers' representatives from large concerns, who opposed official policy, formed their own organization, the Revolutionary Shop Stewards (*Revolutionäre
Obleute*), under the leadership of Richard Müller, first in
Berlin and then in other cities. This organization was to play
an important part both before and during the revolution of
1918.

3. The Revolution of 1918

On 4 August 1914 it had seemed as if the wave of popular
elation had swept away the old antagonism between the
workers and the ruling groups of state and society. But the
struggle to maintain rights attenuated by the needs of the war
effort against further encroachment by the employers (who
used the war as a pretext to reduce the influence of labour
even more than was necessary) soon taught the German
workers that the old class-state had not changed. Their
leaders had no say in government policy, whereas in Britain
labour leaders were members of the war-time government and
of the administration. The government's procrastination on
the issue of electoral reform in Prussia and Ludendorff's military dictatorship seemed to the workers further proof of the
intransigence of the ruling class. Owing to the effect of the
blockade and to an incompetent rationing system, the population had to contend with hunger from the very first winter
of the war. The rationing system favoured the rural population and encouraged a black market which benefited the
well-to-do and the manufacturers of war materials. Though
the army was exempt from the rationing system, the differen-
tial victualling of officers and men (not at the front, but in

the rear, and among the naval personnel in vessels of the High Sea Fleet lying at anchor) caused increasing resentment.

Moreover, everyone was greatly disappointed that the war dragged on and that the anticipated victory did not materialize. The workers felt that the war, which had inflicted such frightful sufferings both at home and at the front, had been lost long ago, and expected a negotiated peace; but the government, the High Command (under Hindenburg and Ludendorff), and the Conservative parties were set on conquest and a victorious outcome of the war. In 1917, instead of making peace in the East, German troops marched into the vast plains of Russia; in 1918, after America's entry into the war and the failure of the intensified submarine campaign, the German High Command, instead of seeking peace, launched a broad offensive in the West. After some initial successes, this offensive led to a total defeat of the German army and, in October 1918, to a request by the High Command (Ludendorff) for a cease-fire.

In the meantime, the emotional patriotism manifested by the German workers in 1914 had long since (at the latest in 1917) given place to an equally emotional pacifism. Since 1917 various strikes were called and protest meetings held in naval establishments. In April 1917, following the so-called "turnip winter", the metal workers in Berlin and other large cities went on strike against a proposed (and subsequently cancelled) reduction of the bread ration; in January 1918 nearly one million workers downed tools all over Germany; in July and August 1918 the miners of Upper Silesia struck for an eight-hour day, pleading physical exhaustion. The first disturbances on board of the large warships anchored off Kiel and Wilhelmshaven took place in 1917, when the pent-up hatred of the class-state turned against the officers; two sailors, Reichpietsch and Kobis, were executed for mutiny. At the end of October 1918, when the High Sea Fleet was ordered to sail against the British Fleet, the sailors refused to obey orders; the war having been lost, they did not want to lay down their lives in a senseless enterprise. This event unleashed the revolution in Germany.

When we examine the course and the aims of the revolutionary movement in Germany during the war, we see that the Spartacists exercised no influence on them. The workers, who were in sympathy with Liebknecht, did not see him as a radical revolutionary, but only as the man whose watchword was "Down with War". Nor could they really distinguish between the Majority Socialists and the Independents. Thus in January 1918, under mass pressure, three leaders from each of the two parties (Ebert, Scheidemann, Braun of the former, and Haase, Ledebour, Dittmann of the latter) were elected to lead the strike. The situation in the Navy was similar : the rioting sailors, who included Catholics and members of the Centre Party, saw no difference between Liebknecht, Scheidemann and Erzberger; Gustav Noske, a Majority Socialist acting on government instructions, was able quickly to gain control of the revolt. The aims of the revolutionary movement also reflected this attitude : they included peace and a bourgeois democracy—but certainly not the overthrow of the government or the proclamation of a republic, even less the establishment of a socialist society.

The demands made by the strikers of January 1918 were : (1) peace without annexation; (2) inclusion of workers' representatives in the peace negotiations; (3) abundant food supplies; (4) lifting of the state of siege; (5) demilitarization of industrial concerns; (6) immediate release of all political prisoners; (7) democratization of the state and electoral reform.

In November 1918 the sailors of the High Sea Fleet demanded an amnesty for all convicted sailors, immunity for those who had taken part in the revolutionary movement ("no adverse comments on the conduct sheet"), the same food for officers and men, a committee to hear complaints from the men, dispensation from having to salute officers except when on duty and from having to address them in the third person.

On 4 November 1918 rioting sailors captured the city of Kiel and, together with the dockers, formed a Workers' and Soldiers' Council with revolutionary powers. By 7 November virtually the whole Fleet had joined the movement which had spread by way of Hamburg across the whole country. On 7 November it reached Munich, on 9 November it spread to Berlin. Emperor William II, who, in the eyes of the rioting workers and soldiers, was the symbol of all disaster, abdicated on the morning of 9 November, and Prince Max von Baden (since 5 October head of a government responsible to parliament) conferred the office of Chancellor upon *Friedrich Ebert* (1871–1925), chairman of the Majority Socialists and leader of their parliamentary group. Soon afterwards *Philipp Scheidemann* (1865–1939), the second most important leader of the Majority Socialists, speaking from a window of the Reichstag building, proclaimed Germany a republic; he thereby forestalled Liebknecht who shortly afterwards proclaimed "the Socialist Republic of Germany" to his followers assembled in the Lustgarten.

While Ebert was negotiating with the leaders of the Independents about the formation of a new government, the Revolutionary Shop Stewards, who had close links with the Spartacists, called a meeting of the Workers' and Soldiers' Councils which decided that on the following morning Councils were to be elected throughout the city and that these Councils would then in the afternoon nominate a government. November 10th was a Sunday; at 3 p.m. some 3,000 representatives of Berlin Soldiers' and Workers' Councils assembled in the Busch Circus. It became evident that the followers of the Majority Socialists were in the majority; the government, which had been formed in the meantime (SPD: Ebert, Scheidemann, Landsberg; USPD: Haase, Dittmann; Revolutionary Shop Stewards: Barth) was approved as the Council of the People's Commissars. At the same time the Action Committee of Soldiers' and Workers' Councils, which was to watch over the government, was nominated on a parity basis. Ebert had won, but in terms of actual power his victory was not yet secure. However, on the evening of 10 November he received a telephone call from Groener, the new Quartermaster General, who informed him that the army was at the new government's disposal to avert civil war on condition that Ebert and his Ministers maintained peace and order, and safeguarded military discipline and the authority of the officers.

At the National Congress of the Workers' and Soldiers' Councils which met in Berlin from 16 to 19 December, the Majority Socialists were able to overcome the opposition of those who advocated a "Republic of Councils", and to pass a resolution demanding the election of a National Assembly which would determine the form and character of the new parliamentary republic.

When a few days later a division of the People's Marines, who had come to Berlin from Cuxhaven in early November to protect the revolutionary government, mutinied, Ebert called in troops of the old army; thereupon the Independents resigned from the government; Noske and Wissell (1869–1962) joined the Council of People's Commissars. At the same time the Spartacus group split away from the Independents; and at the end of December, led by Rosa Luxemburg and Karl Liebknecht, they formed the Communist Party of Germany (*Kommunistische Partei Deutschlands*-KPD). During the first days of January new disorders—the so-called Spartacus rising —took place in Berlin. Followers of the KPD (though not Rosa Luxemburg), some Revolutionary Shop Stewards, and local branches of the USPD felt that the time had come to overthrow the government. Noske organized Free Corps and with their help crushed the rising on 10 and 11 January, 1919. On 15 January Rosa Luxemburg and Karl Liebknecht were murdered by soldiers of the Free Corps. A wave of strikes, disorders and uprisings now spread across Germany. In Munich a Republic of Soviets (*Räte-Republik*) was proclaimed which lasted from 7 April to 2 May. The Free Corps, who were now government troops, intervened everywhere : meanwhile the National Assembly, elected on 19 January and convened at Weimar on 6 February, deliberated about the Constitution of the new German republic.

For the leaders of the Majority Socialists who were now in power, the revolution had ended on 10 November 1918. They had wanted neither a revolution nor a republic. In an endeavour to direct the revolutionary movement into constitutional and lawful channels, Ebert and his collaborators concentrated on convening a National Assembly with the least possible delay. The programme of the People's Commissars (including the USPD) was therefore to include two stages : first, administrative and economic machinery must be set up again to safeguard the existence of the state and the country; only after this had been done could they aspire to a new, social-democratic state made possible by a democratic constitution. The re-establishment of "peace and order" could only

be achieved with the help of the old authoritarian bureaucracy and of the imperial army with whom the representatives of the revolutionary movement had entered into a kind
of alliance on the very first day of the revolution. The trade
unions of all shades of opinion met the employers' associations
on 15 November to set up a working group on the basis of an
agreement which admittedly gave the trade unions all that
they had demanded for decades—e.g. an eight-hour day and
the unrestricted right to organize—and gained them official
recognition by the state and the employers; but it robbed
them of every chance of intervening in the structure of the
economy.

In November 1918 it became obvious that the leaders of
the Social Democrats lacked a constructive democratic,
socialist conception of state and society which would have
enabled them to utilize the revolutionary situation. Yet their
ability to create a new order had been their proudest boast
during the decades of their opposition to the old system. By
now the new socialist system had at best come to mean
"unrestricted political freedom" and "social security". (Cf.
Programme of the Council of People's Commissars, 12
November, 1918.)

During 1918 and 1919 the leadership of the SPD fought
hard to gain recognition for its policies among its own rank
and file by pleading, in all sincerity, that the party was
struggling to save Germany from Bolshevism. This plea was
to prove fatal for the future destiny of the Republic and for
the attitude of the workers towards their new state. It rested
on a politically unrealistic assessment of the situation : the
opponents of parliamentary democracy were ideologically and
numerically too weak and too disunited to have any chance
of success; beyond this, the fight against the Workers' and
Soldiers' Councils deprived the leaders of the Social Democrats
of a reliable tool for the establishment and maintenance of
democratic practices in the administration.

The majority of the USPD agreed with the Majority Socialists
that the political goal was a parliamentary democracy. The
USPD wanted no more than to postpone convening the
National Assembly for a few months during which the
nationalization of the basic industries and the democratiza-

tion of the administrative machine could be carried out. They parted from the SPD and became more radical only after it had been decided to use the old imperial army against the Left-wing opponents of the provisional government (December 1918). During the months of the revolution the Workers' and Soldiers' Councils, whose sympathies were in the main with the Majority Socialists, confined their activities primarily to the maintenance of order; they functioned as liaison between the population and the administration, and their aim was to introduce a democratic system into the administration. In 1918–19 the Workers' Councils were not merely the only available, but also the most suitable instruments to enable the workers, who had come "of age" in November, to gain positions of power in the administration and thus to make sure that the young republic would be democratic in character. The aim of the massive Ruhr Workers' Movement of 1919 (which was later crushed by force) was merely "socialization", by which they meant the introduction of co-determination in industry and its maintenance by works councils. The Revolutionary Shop Stewards, who formed the Left wing of the USPD and collaborated with the Spartacists, were probably the most consistent proponents of a Soviet-style system of Councils. But their influence was both geographically and organizationally limited; they later refused an invitation to join the KPD. Among the members of the Spartacus League (later KPD) Rosa Luxemburg, a genuine disciple of Marx and Engels, sharply criticized Lenin. In her "Russian Revolution" of 1918 she says: "It is the historical task of the proletariat, when it has gained power, to create a socialist democracy in place of a bourgeois democracy, and not to abolish democracy altogether". The revolution meant to her not a single blow, but a series of long, tenacious engagements of the proletariat which was not initially aware of its strength and tasks. This view, which she shared with a small circle of followers, in some ways contradicted the opinions held by the majority of utopian radicals, who believed that with the establishment of the Workers' Councils the ultimate goal—a dictatorship of the Soviets—was within their grasp, and that this could be achieved by a policy of coups. Both Rosa Luxemburg and Karl Liebknecht were affected by the dichotomy between the belief in the historical law of economic development and the will to revolutionary action; this led them to the assumption that the masses were rapidly becoming more radical, and tempted them to use corresponding tactics. Thus in 1918–19 the Spartacists also were at odds with political reality; they completely misinterpreted the "revolutionary" masses and made this misinterpretation into a corner-stone of their tactics in the struggle for power.

In 1918–19 the German Social Democrats were unable to create the social and ideological foundations for the new state; their party had no clear conception of a social-democratic policy which would embrace all the aspects of state and society. It remained enmeshed in ideas of government which were inspired by a monarchic and authoritarian system. The gulf between the great utopia of a socialist society and the disillusioned reality of a defeated, starving and shattered nation seemed to inhibit any activity beyond the immediate needs of the day. In any case, dependence upon the imperial army and civil service left little elbow room for the realization of new ideas. Yet the seemingly unavoidable alternative between a bolshevist dictatorship and an alliance with the imperial bureaucracy and army might have been removed by an attempt—based on a frank assessment of the situation —at influencing the groups disqualified because of their bolshevist and anti-democratic character. A third possibility might have emerged: "a new republic of the common people" (Arthur Rosenberg, *"History"* and *"Entstehung"*).

Thus the revolution of 1918 emerges as a chance which had been missed. The workers either turned away from their leaders in disappointment; or they remained faithful to them without understanding them. The leaders had manoeuvred themselves into a political predicament from which there was no escape.

CHAPTER VI

1919–1930

1. Economic and Social Conditions in the Weimar Republic

Since the events of November 1918 did not change the structure of the German society, they can hardly be called a social revolution; within a few years the old ruling class re-established its pre-eminence in the government, the economy and the society, though up to 1923 this fact was largely obscured by a series of political and economic crises. During its first years the republic lived on the brink of a precarious existence; the events of that period included the Versailles Peace Treaty (implemented after January 1920), the Kapp *Putsch* (March 1920), attempted communist uprisings in the Ruhr and in Central Germany (March–April 1920, and March 1921), the assassination of Erzberger (August 1921) and of Rathenau (June 1922), the inflation (culminating in autumn 1923), the Ruhr Struggle (1923), and the Hitler *Putsch* (November 1923). However, the stabilization of the currency (November 1923), the scaling down of reparation payments by the Dawes Plan (August 1924), and Gustav Stresemann's foreign policy of step-by-step agreement (in September 1926 Germany was admitted to the League of Nations) finally led to a period of recovery which lasted till the end of 1929.

As soon as conditions became more stable the hitherto disguised supremacy of the old Prussian aristocracy, the government bureaucracy, the feudalized upper-class bourgeoisie and the military became evident. It was most strikingly symbolized by the election, in 1925, of Paul von Hindenburg, the defeated Field-Marshal of the old imperial army, to the Presidency of the young republic. The diplomats and generals, the officials and ministers, many industrialists and party leaders were once again drawn from the ranks of the ruling classes of the defunct Empire. In spite of the fact that the

Weimar Republic abolished all social privileges and political pretensions of the former ruling classes, the values and behaviour patterns of the old monarchic and authoritarian system prevailed again. They included the patriarchal, authoritarian family structure, the militaristic, authoritarian organization of industrial concerns, the hierarchic, authoritarian order of social precedence; the distance separating "above and below" characterized the relationship between citizen and government.

The democratic, parliamentary system of government in the Weimar Republic lacked the foundation of a corresponding social structure. From the very beginning, anti-democratic, autocratic elements were appointed to some of the positions of power which they finally came to dominate completely and exclusively. These elements regarded parliamentary democracy as a system operated by bureaucrats, swayed by plebiscites, and constitutionally authoritarian; accordingly, they used the machinery of democracy to corrupt the original democratic and social intentions of the founders of the republic. The rare instances in which a start was made to render the economy more democratic lagged sadly behind the expectations raised by the Constitution.

Though it was originally intended to socialize at least the key-industries, this did not, in practice, go beyond the creation of self-governing corporations in the coal-mining, potash-mining and steel industries. In the steel industry self-government was soon abolished, but in the other two industries it survived till the end of the republic. Since the employers and employees, who between them constituted a majority on the boards of these corporations, frequently fixed wages and prices at the expense of the consumer, the government often had to exercise its vetoing power to protect the consumer. Thus the self-government in fact meant nothing but a state-controlled coercive monopoly. Before 1914 collective agreements about rates of pay were regarded as purely private arrangements between the representatives of the employers and the workers; in the Weimar Republic the collective labour contract was regarded as a legally binding normal labour agreement. In 1913 some two million workers were covered by wage agreements; in 1919 this figure had risen to almost six million, in 1928 to over 12 million. Only free and independent unions had the right to represent the workers in collective bargaining. The state reserved the right to mediate in difficult negotiations, to declare wage agreements generally binding, and to enforce its own decision where no agreement was reached (compulsory arbitration).

The Works Council Law of February 1920 was the result of an attempt by the leaders of the SPD and the trade unions to curb the Workers' Council movement. It laid down that in all establishments with at least five employees one delegate was to be elected annually; for establishments with more than twenty employees, the annual election of a works council became obligatory. However, the double task imposed on the works councils proved extremely difficult, if not altogether impossible; they were to "look after the common economic interests of the employees (workers and other staff) vis à vis the employer", and, at the same time, "support the employer in the fulfilment of the establishment's purpose" (cf. *lex sit.*, § 1.). The works councils were e.g. entitled to inspect the books of the company, and to voting rights on the boards of directors. Difficulties not only arose from the attitude of the employers and the inadequate training of the members of the works councils, but were inherent in the problem which the law tried to solve : a consistent commitment to the interests of the workers could not easily be reconciled with the concern for managerial tasks entirely directed towards the promotion of the company's interests. The generally recognized favourable effects of the Works Council Law relate, therefore, mainly to those areas of the works councils' activity where, in their role of "the long arm of the trade unions", they negotiated and supervised wage agreements, or where, as "links" or "buffers" between employers and employees, they acted as mediators in internal disputes. The Weimar Constitution also provided for the setting up of national works councils and national economic councils (Article 165), but only the latter actually came into being : their activities were not very meaningful.

After the stabilization of the currency and the adoption of the Dawes Plan, the German economy entered upon a period of recovery which in its extent and strength surpassed all precedents. This was due to two factors : the improvement of production methods to meet the requirements of a highly developed capitalist economy (rationalization), and a big influx of foreign, mainly American, capital.

> The rationalization enabled Germany to recapture its leading position in the chemical, electrical and optical industries, and to some extent also in textiles and machine construction. As early as 1926 German exports reached their pre-war level; by 1929 they exceeded the level of 1913 by 34 per cent (in spite of territorial losses in Europe and the loss of colonies). The foreign credits not only rebuilt the German economy; they were also used to pay the German reparation debts.

The economic recovery was accompanied by a new wave of industrial mergers.

> While the approximate total capital of the 12,400 (officially registered) joint-stock companies amounted to some 20,000 million marks, a total of 13,250 million marks was distributed among a mere 2,000 companies. Combines accounted for 93 per cent of the mining industry, 96 per cent of the dye industry, 95 per cent of the steel industry and 87 per cent of the electrical industry. The giant *IG-Farben* (*IG-Dyes*) and the *Vereinigte Stahlwerke* (United Steel Co.) also came into being at that time.

In order to avert the threat of socialization, the employers formed a working group with the trade unions, but this broke up in 1924. The employers remained convinced that a system based on private capital which gives free play to economic forces is the best of all possible economic systems; they were prepared to accept a limited amount of social policy as a necessary corrective.

The period from 1919 to 1933 is characterized by a further growth of the numbers of persons employed, both manual workers and other staff; in particular, the war-time employment of women in industry and commerce continued. During the inflation the level of wages and salaries sank far below the worst pre-war levels, but this was quickly remedied after the stabilization of the currency.

In 1928 the average real wages of all employed and unemployed persons were no higher than those of 1913–14; but wages varied greatly from industry to industry, being generally higher in booming industries and trades (plasterers, metal workers), and in those branches of the economy where the unions were traditionally strong (printing).

The eight-hour day was regarded by the workers as one of the most important achievements of the revolution. It is typical of the balance of power in the new republic that its introduction became the most controversial of the new measures. And when it came to its practical application the employers' point of view made itself felt; thus in October 1926 53 per cent of the officially registered 750,000 workers worked more than 48 hours per week; of these 50 per cent worked a 52–54 hours week. These abuses were not curbed till an emergency law about working hours to some extent reduced excessive overtime in 1927.

The extension of the social security provisions promised in November 1918 was at first vitiated by the inflation. But after 1923 the existing system of insurance was liberally expanded, and in 1927 broadened to include unemployment insurance.

Even at the peak of the boom in 1927–28 unemployment was higher than during the pre-war periods of depression. While in the early years of the Weimar Republic high unemployment figures were due to demobilization, after 1923 they were caused by rationalization, which was carried out with no thought of its social consequences. Consumption did not keep pace with increased production; moreover monopolistic price agreements left prices virtually unchanged, so that demand was not stimulated by lower prices even when wages rose.

Unemployment figures (for all occupations) read as follows: early 1919 : 1 million; middle 1919 : ½ million; middle 1920 : ¼ million; early 1921 : 400,000; end of 1921 : 150,000; 1922 : 120,000; middle 1923 : 140,000; winter 1923–24 : 1·25 million; 1924 : 400,000; 1925 : 200,000; early 1926 : 2 million; middle 1926 : 1·25 million; 1927 : 350,000; 1928 : 600,000; middle 1929 (beginning of crisis) : 1·25 million; middle 1930 : 2·76 million; middle 1931; 3·99 million; February 1932 : 6·12 million; middle 1932 : 5·39 million; January 1933 : 6·13 million.

After the political and economic situation had become

more stable, the working conditions of both manual and non-manual workers were determined by the effects of rationalization. Industrial concerns introduced increasingly complicated machines and tools, and production processes were mechanized (e.g. conveyor belt assembly). As a consequence workers trained for one special process were given preference over skilled workers and auxiliary unskilled labour. The new production methods meant that the individual came to enjoy his work less, and became more concerned with leisure; mechanization made it easier to change one's employment, but working conditions remained virtually unchanged. Efforts towards a measure of welfare policy within individual concerns were intended to bind the worker to "his" firm. In non-manual occupations the pre-war concept of individual skill and performance was also being replaced by mechanization and division of labour which again favoured young employees and particularly female labour. There was hardly any difference between manual workers and other (low and medium grade) employees as far as working conditions and rates of pay were concerned.

2. *The SPD and the KPD in the Weimar Republic*

The events of November 1918 had fundamentally changed the position of the SPD compared with the period before the war; formerly excluded from any responsible collaboration with the government and with no social standing, it now became the power responsible for the state and of crucial importance to it. In the elections to the National Assembly the two socialist parties obtained only 45·5 per cent of the votes, i.e. not a clear mandate for a transformation of the state and the society along socialist lines. Faithful to the principles which they had enunciated before the revolution, namely that they would await, and abide by, the majority decision of the people, the Social Democrats (without the Independents) entered into a coalition with the German Democratic Party and the Centre Party to build a new state.

The Constitution adopted on 19 August 1919 left open many questions about the future distribution and administration of power, particularly in the economic and social spheres.

Bound to its coalition partners (1919–20 and 1921–22 to the Democrats and the Centre Party, 1923 and 1928–30 also to the German People's Party), or forced into opposition (1920, 1924–28), the SPD (from 1922 reunited with the Right wing of the USPD) proved incapable of exploiting the political potential of the workers' organizations on many occasions which offered themselves during that period : e.g. when framing the Enabling Law on Socializing and the Works Councils; after the Kapp *Putsch* of 1920; at the presidential elections of 1925, when, in the second ballot, the party prematurely withdrew its candidate, Otto Braun, in favour of the Centre Party's candidate, Marx; and again in 1928 when—emerging as the strongest party—the SPD formed a government.

The reluctance of the Social Democrats to exploit their own powerful position had two causes: the first, which became obvious as early as 1918–19 and was so fatally confirmed after 1930, stemmed from their distaste for other than parliamentary methods; the second from their inability to transform the revolutionary mood prevailing among the workers and among large sections of the middle class into political action. At several junctures in the life of the Weimar Republic it would have been possible to pursue an active, militant policy, e.g. in 1922 after the assassination of Rathenau; in 1923 at the height of the Ruhr Struggle which the employers used to launch a general offensive against the social and political gains of the workers; when force was used against Saxony and Thuringia to execute federal orders; or in 1926, when a plebiscite was held on the question of the princes being expropriated without compensation—this being, incidentally, the only time, apart from the Kapp *Putsch,* when the two workers' parties joined together for common action. All these opportunities were missed. Moreover, the leaders of the SPD, while sharing in the responsibilities of government, continued to pursue their policy of "defence against Bolshevism", launched in 1918. The Communist Party's provocative and aggressive attitude towards the republic, and its growing power to attract the workers gave this line of policy added impetus. It led the Social Democratic leaders to regard revolutionary feelings and political disorders among the workers invariably as symptoms of Communism;

it did not occur to them that other motives or attitudes could be at work. This revealed the core of their programme: peace and order, the safeguarding of the republic, and the achievement of the greatest possible progress under the given circumstances of power distribution. Wilhelm Keil said at the congress of the SPD in Heidelberg in 1925 :

> We Social Democrats feel ourselves to be the real representatives of the democratic republic, and we must, therefore, defend it with all our might... In essence, the Social Democrats are, and remain, the advocate of the poor, the workers and the disinherited. We must use all our power in public life to defend the vital interests of the working people and of the innocent victims of the capitalist economy against the patronage of property. Thus, when we are in opposition, our demands must not exceed those limits which we would have to honour if we were in power.

Such a concept of politics all too often caused the party leaders to be content with small concrete achievements and to overestimate the opponents' resistance. Coupled with a lack of boldness and a growing desire for security, this led to the danger of a self-satisfied stagnating opportunism.

After the SPD had relinquished the aim of changing the structure of the state, the economy and the society, its successes in the Weimar Republic were confined to the sphere of social policy, in which they had traditionally been active; here, their achievements were impressive, thanks to their tireless and tenacious efforts in parliament. It is remarkable that, like the trade unions, they failed to recognize the problematic nature of the "borrowed prosperity" (a prosperity founded on Germany's indebtedness abroad); their main concern was that the workers should have the greatest possible share in it.

An account of the achievements of the German Social Democrats would be incomplete without a mention of the Prussian concept of their policy. Apart from some minor interruptions, Prussia was governed from 1919 onwards by a social-democratic Prime Minister—Paul Hirsch, and from 1920 *Otto Braun*, (1872–1955)—and a social-democratic Minister of the Interior—*Carl Severing*, (1875–1952), and

Albert Grzesinski. Here in Prussia, the Social Democrats tried to create a model republican national state; according to their political ideas, this meant perfectly functioning and correctly administered democratic institutions. Just as Bismarck had once conquered the Empire from Prussia, so the German Social Democrats—in proportion as their influence waned in the central government—hoped to recapture the republic from their Prussian bastion. The Prussian concept of the SPD eventually became more important than the idea of a unified national administration advocated by the party since 1918. The SPD also exercised a decisive influence on the government and administration of Baden, Hesse, and Hamburg. (In 1929 the SPD captured more than a third of all the seats in the Land diets.)

Thousands of German cities had social-democratic mayors and municipal councils; in the large towns and in industrial regions—the "red islands in the capitalist sea"—the SPD was particularly successful in promoting a progressive local government policy. But this successful practical work for the republic at the Land and municipal levels lacked a theoretical foundation and was, therefore, carried out with what almost amounted to a bad conscience.

Unlike all the other democratic parties, the SPD tried consistently and unequivocally to inculcate in all citizens an awareness of their binding duties to the republican state. Its efforts failed; the leaders of the party had equated democracy with the perfect functioning of democratic institutions and with the absolute legal integrity of those who upheld them.

The efforts of the social-democratic leaders to make the republic democratic were hampered by yet another factor: the very elements who should have been attacked by the Social Democrats for being insufficiently committed to republican ideals were instrumental, during the years of stabilization, in raising Germany once more to the position of a great power, and the social-democratic leaders, even though themselves unable to play a leading part in bringing this about, considered the country's rise to power vitally important. The situation was very similar to that in which the party found itself before 1914; as before, it manifested a thoroughly loyal attitude towards the international labour movement. In 1919 the Second International was revived once again; in 1923 the Labour and Socialist International was founded; the Third (Communist) International came into being in 1919. What appeared outwardly as a lack of a single purpose was—as it had been during that earlier period—an expression of divided loyalties: loyalty to the national state on the one hand, and, on the other, loyalty to the international working class to whose cause the Social Democrats felt themselves equally committed by tradition.

The ambivalent policies of the SPD are reflected in election figures and in the inner structure of the party.

The party's policies both during and after the revolution were responsible for the loss of working class votes in 1920 and again in May 1924; this loss was never recovered. The aim of drawing all workers into the SPD was not achieved; the catholic workers remained on the whole faithful to the Centre Party; the protestant workers, insofar as they were organized in the Christian Trade Unions, voted for the bourgeois-nationalist parties. The additional votes for the SPD in 1928 and 1930 (as compared with 1924) came mainly from the reservoir of the disintegrating German Democratic Party; this was partly true also as regards increases in membership.

The influence of the SPD among the agricultural workers (particularly in the Eastern provinces of Prussia) remained slight, as it had been before the war. The party was favoured neither by the small farmers nor by the lower middle class; nor did many members of the proletarianized non-manual workers join the party (in contrast to the lower ranks of the civil service). Young people also felt less attracted to the party than had been expected. Though the SPD was no longer a purely working-class party, it certainly had not become a genuine people's party. The labour movement's increasingly bourgeois tendencies—a resumption of a trend noticeable even before 1914—were not due to the fact that the movement had opened its doors to the middle class, but rather to the workers' improved standard of living, and to the greater opportunities which now offered themselves for social advancement.

Election year		Number of votes (million)		Proportion of votes in per cent	Seats
	1919	SPD	11·5	37·9	163
		USPD	2·3	7·6	22
	1920	SPD	6·1	21·6	102
		USPD	5·0	18·0	84
May	1924	SPD	6·0	20·5	100
Dec.	1924	SPD	7·9	26·0	131
	1928	SPD	9·1	29·8	153
	1930	SPD	8·5	24·5	143
June	1932	SPD	7·9	21·6	133
Nov.	1932	SPD	7·2	20·4	121
March	1933	SPD	7·2	18·3	120

Membership figures of the SPD

	Year	Men	Women	Total
Early	1920	973,201	207,007	1,180,208
Early	1925	537,109	153,693	690,902
Early	1930	803,442	218,335	1,021,777
End	1931	778,622	230,331	1,008,953

Of a total of over a million members in 1930 60 per cent
were manual workers (1926 : 73 per cent), 10 per cent non-
manual workers, 3 per cent civil servants, 17 per cent housewives. Before the war only 10 per cent of members were not
manual workers. In 1930 8 per cent of the members were
under 25 years of age, and 25.9 per cent over 60.

Though facing new tasks imposed upon it by its share in
the responsibilities of government, the SPD was still dominated by traditional attitudes; this is most clearly demonstrated
by the fact that the inherited principles of party organization
remained unchanged; the organizational structure retained
the character which it had acquired when it had stood in
opposition to an authoritarian monarchy : bureaucratically
reliable and run with almost military precision, it was militant
and always ready to do battle. The social antecedents (predominantly artisan and skilled worker) and the professional
career of the party's officers (a slow rise from the ranks)
remained unchanged; the increasingly frequent taunts from
the extreme Right and Left that the organization was turning
into a "system of big wigs" were largely based on demagogic

exaggeration : with a membership of more than one million, the party bureaucracy was only 10,000 strong. The stability of its organization and the solidity of its party machine gave the SPD a great advantage over the other democratic parties. It meant that conflicts could be solved more easily, breaches avoided and defeats overcome. But these advantages were gained at the expense of adaptability in both tactical and strategic questions of policy, and this in turn militated against a systematic analysis of the development which had begun in 1918. The SPD's inner structure always retained the character of a closed party representing a specific class, a party with essentially working class connotations. There is no doubt that the social and political mentality of the bulk of its members and followers exercised a determining influence on its character.

For many of the workers who had been brought up as Social Democrats the Weimar Republic was a great disappointment. The sanctions imposed on Germany by its wartime enemies, and the resulting economic crises could be regarded as necessary consequences of the old system and the lost war; but the internal political situation was seen as a victory for the counter-revolution and a defeat of the revolutionary forces. The democratic republic, the great goal of the labour movement since its inception, was greeted with enthusiasm in 1918–19, because it held the promise of Socialism being put into practice or at least of a tangible and lasting improvement in the economic, social and political situation of the workers. In the event, the Weimar Republic did not, so it seemed to the workers, abolish the traditional pre-eminence of the old ruling classes—the army, bureaucracy, aristocracy and upper-middle class; it did not free the workers from economic insecurity and did not put an end to social injustices. In 1922–23, when the inflation and the Ruhr Struggle were at their height, the mood of the workers became so revolutionary that it seems safe to assume (as did A. Rosenberg in his "History of the German Republic") that, in the summer of 1923, the majority of the German workers were in sympathy with the German Communist Party; but this revolutionary mood found no echo in the KPD or in any of the other parties.

However, in the face of the declining social status of the working class and their political disunity, most workers considered a new revolution or even an actively militant policy out of the question; this conviction introduced a strong note of resignation into their political mentality. Their social self-confidence had also diminished compared with the pre-war period when they could, at least, still project their wishes into the future. To be a worker meant less than ever, and the eagerness to achieve a higher social status—which now mainly meant to become a non-manual worker—was so great that the actual proletarian existence and the waning social prestige of the non-manual workers went quite unnoticed.

Yet the great majority of the German workers, including even the bitterly disappointed ones, held fast to their old organizations, where suspicion and political listlessness were mitigated by long established party discipline. Above all, the organizations of the labour movement protected the worker against economic insecurity and social decline; they offered familiar shelter, where common activities and a community of interest helped to relieve the oppressive feeling of social and political discrimination.

Not till towards the end of the period of stabilization did the workers seem to regain a measure of confidence in the state, and some hope that it might yet be possible to find an approach by which to fashion the republic into a state of their own. After 1930, the threat to the republic from Right- and Left-wing extremist groups made it even more obvious that the democracy of 1918 constituted, in spite of its imperfections, a most valuable basis for the workers' struggle for political and social equality.

During the Weimar Republic, the SPD's organization was expanded and perfected so that it might continue to fulfil the principal tasks of a party whose particular concern was the integration of a specific stratum of the population.

The following organizational developments took place : the foundation of Labour Welfare (*Arbeiterwohlfahrt*) as a voluntary mutual aid association (1919–20). The creation of the National Committee for Socialist Education (after 1919); the linking up of all cultural bodies of the labour movement into the Socialist Cultural Union (1923). Development of youth organizations: the National Committee of Young Socialists (1919) for party members over 18 (after 1927 over 20); the Socialist League of Youth (1922), a merger of the youth organizations of the SPD and the USPD for adolescents between the ages of 14 and 18 (later 20); the Socialist Children's Association (1923). Organizations for academics: for teachers (1919), lawyers (1925), physicians (1926), university students (1931); the last mentioned organization was to help social-democratic students and to further scientific co-operation. The SPD played an important part in the founding of the *Reichsbanner,* an organization of republican veterans; also of the Iron Front (1931), a militant republican organization with a membership of about 10 million, drawn from the SPD, the workers' sports organizations, trade unions and the veterans' organization. Its symbol were three arrows. Social-democratic press: in 1929—203 papers, of which 74 had a national circulation; 129 publishing houses and 107 presses.

The top echelon of the SPD (the party's executive and the parliamentary party) also hardly changed its structure. As far back as the turn of the century, the tribune-of-the-people type of men, like Bebel and Liebknecht, had been superseded by a new generation of leaders, distinguished by their reliability and realism, men like Friedrich Ebert and *Hermann Müller* (1876–1931); Müller replaced Ebert as party chairman in 1919; he became Reich Chancellor in 1920 and again from 1928 to 1930. These men, however, often lacked political imagination and daring, and the necessary insight into people's changed political susceptibilities. Originally skilled workers or artisans, most of them had reached the higher ranks of the party after working for the party press or the trade unions. During the Weimar Republic this well-defined artisan type exercised a particularly strong influence on the party and strengthened the German worker's ever present tendency to imitate the middle class. As professional politicians, these men possessed a great deal of experience acquired during their many years in the party and in politics generally; this and the party's tendency to appoint for life led to a situation where the top leadership tended to be dominated by the older generation, though the chances afforded to gifted young politicians were, on the whole, better than before the war.

The new programme, adopted by the SPD Congress at

Görlitz in 1921, avoided the use of marxist terminology and tried to extend its appeal to non-proletarian strata of the population. ("The German Social Democratic Party is the party of the working people in town and country.") It thus seemed to complete the SPD's development into a party of national and social reform also on the programmatic level.

The practical part of the programme was abrogated as early as 1922 in consequence of the merger of the SPD and the USPD; in 1925, at the Congress in Heidelberg, the whole programme was scrapped. It was replaced by the Heidelberg Programme which harked back to the Erfurt Programme of 1891. Its basis was an economic analysis of existing conditions which revealed the increasing concentration and the growing power of capital, the "ever acuter contrast between the exploiters and the exploited", the "increasingly bitter class struggle between the capitalist rulers of the economy and those whom they rule", and the numerical growth of the proletariat (including non-manual workers and graduates). The programme proposed that—within the constitutional framework of the democratic republic—a systematic policy of reform and the capture of political power by the workers should lead to the socialization of the means of production as a precondition of a socialist society.

> The goal of the working class can only be achieved by transforming the capitalist private ownership of the means of production into social ownership. When capitalist production is replaced by socialist production by the people for the people, then the growth and development of productive forces will become the source of great prosperity and universal betterment. Only then will society, in harmony and solidarity, rise from its subjection to blind economic forces and from general disintegration, and achieve free self-government.

This might have served as an answer to the workers who, brought up in the tradition of the old revolutionary phraseology, wondered about the meaning of the developments since 1918 and how they would lead to Socialism. But the programme failed to tackle two tasks which the events of 1918 had brought into focus: it did not provide the necessary theoretical clarification of basic concepts, such as internationalism, state, democracy and the class struggle; nor did it give a concrete sociological analysis of the power relations in the state. The old rift between theory and practice continued to be manifest also during the Weimar Republic: on the one hand the SPD still proclaimed its determination to transform the class state and the bourgeois-capitalist society into a socialist order; on the other hand it actively exerted its influence on the state in the interest of the workers in order to reform a system which, by implication, it regarded as thoroughly worthy of reformation.

It fell to the party's theoreticians to try and bridge the gulf between theory and practice, to reconcile Right- and Left-wing opinions within the party, and, at the same time, to undermine the case of the KPD agitators. They attempted to do this by acknowledging the actual, bourgeois-capitalist nature of the republic, but giving it a revolutionary-socialist (marxist) interpretation. This approach was adopted by e.g. *Rudolf Hilferding* (1877–1941), who succeeded Kautsky as the party's leading theoretician; he stated that the democratic republic was the only system within which the working class could achieve its immediate goal, namely the capture of decisive political power. In the same vein he interpreted capitalist cartels and combines as a preliminary step towards a planned, socialist economy; it was he who at the SPD's Congress at Kiel in 1927 coined the slogan: "Make the entire working class into a political party"; this slogan was, in fact, only meant to say that the SPD wanted to win over the workers who were tied to denominational organizations, particularly those who voted for the Centre Party; and this in turn implied that the same economic situation is bound to lead to the same political action. Certain sections on the Right as well as on the Left of the party opposed this new version of the Kautskyan integrationist ideology on the grounds that it was a pseudo-revolutionary, purely verbal radicalism which tended to obscure the real state of affairs and led to stagnation and opportunism.

The Left rallied round the journals *"Klassenkampf"* (1927), edited by Max Seydewitz, Kurt Rosenfeld, Heinrich Ströbel and Max Adler (the theoretician of Austrian Marxism), and *"Sozialistische Politik und Wirtschaft"* (1923), edited by Dr. Paul Levi; the two journals merged in 1928. Among this group originated the Socialist Workers' Party (*Sozialistische Arbeiter-*

partei—SAP) which split away from the SPD in 1931. The International League of Youth (*Internationaler Jugend-Bund-IJB*) founded by the Göttingen philosopher and mathematician Leonard Nelson, held consistently rationalist (anti-marxist) views and consequently deplored the SPD's conformist policy, and aspired to an alliance with the strictly marxist and pacifist Left-wing opposition. The group was first expelled from the Socialist League of Youth (in 1925) and later from the party. Its successor (*Internationaler Sozialistischer Kampf-Bund* ISK), which, like the SAP, was to prove its worth when it actively defended the republic and fought against the extremists on the Right. The Right wing of the SPD was organizationally weaker and showed less cohesion but it also tried to give the SPD a new theoretical and practical direction; an example is the Hofgeismar Group of Young Socialists (1923), who demanded a national orientation in politics and national unity; the most influential figures of this movement were Hermann Heller, Gustav Radbruch, Paul Natorp and Hendrik de Man. A group of younger reformists (Carlo Mierendorff, Theodor Haubach, Julius Leber) opposed the revolutionary radicalism of the Left as well as the liberal-democratic reformism of the party's leadership; they hoped to revive the senescent party and the menaced republic by action based on militantly democratic convictions and by an emotional commitment to democracy. This group gained a certain significance only during the last stage of the republic. The Religious Socialists occupied a special position; though they formed a separate group outside the SPD, most of them gave their political allegiance to it. Under the leadership of the protestant minister Erwin Eckert and of Emil Fuchs, this group was consistently pacifist and close to the radical Left. (As a protest against the SPD's policy of tolerance, Eckert later joined the KPD.) A circle whose interests lay in theoretical rather than practical politics collected round the protestant professors *Paul Tillich* (1886–1965), Eduard Heimann and Carl Mennicke. Though this circle agreed in principle with the ideas expressed in the Heidelberg Programme, its attitude became gradually more critical towards it. The total number of Religious Socialists was estimated at about 25–30,000. At the beginning of 1929, there came into existence another small group of Catholic Socialists led by Heinrich Mertens.

Among the most important theoretical works about Socialism

published at the time of the Weimar Republic we may name the following: Max Adler, *"Marxistische Probleme"*, 5th edition 1922; Max Adler, *"Der Marxismus als proletarische Lebenslehre"*, 3rd ed. 1930; Rudolf Hilferding, *"Das Finanzkapital"*, 2nd ed. 1923; Fritz Sternberg, *"Der Imperialismus"*, 1st ed. 1926; Otto Bauer, *"Kapitalismus und Sozialismus nach dem Weltkriege"*, 1931; Eduard Heimann, *"Soziale Theorie des Kapitalismus"*, 1929; Eduard Heimann, *"Kapitalismus und Sozialismus"*, 1931; Gustav Radbruch, *"Kulturlehre des Sozialismus"*, 1922; Hermann Heller, *"Sozialismus und Nation"*, 1924; Hendrik de Man, *"Psychology of Socialism"*, London, 1928.

Between 1919 and 1930 the SPD did not consistently follow either the revolutionary-socialist or the liberal-democratic path. Its aim remained unchanged: to fight for "the spiritual, political and economic emancipation of the toiling masses"; yet it failed to imprint its character on the republic which enjoyed the support of the majority of the population, and to bring about political *as well as* social democracy.

The KPD was even less successful in achieving its objectives, namely to win the support of the German workers and to establish a dictatorship of the proletariat in place of the democratic republic. At the time of its foundation, at the end of December 1918, the KPD consisted of a small minority of workers and intellectuals; the members of the syndicalist extreme Left, who advocated an immediate revolutionary proletarian uprising, overruled the leaders (Liebknecht, Luxemburg) at the very first Party Congress, and refused to take part in the elections for the National Assembly. After the murder of the two leaders, the party fell under the sway of the extreme Left, till Paul Levi (who later rejoined the SPD via the USPD), who represented the Right, took over the party leadership in the autumn of 1919. The following spring there ensued a complete rupture with the extreme Left who formed themselves into the Communist Workers' Party of Germany (*Kommunistische Arbeiterpartei Deutschlands—* KAPD). Though this move cost the KPD half its members, a merger with the Left wing of the USPD now became a practical possibility; it became a fact after the USPD's Congress at Halle in October 1920. (The rest of the USPD rejoined the SPD in 1922, while a small group, led by Georg Ledebour and Theodor Liebknecht, retained the identity of the USPD; Ledebour was expelled from the USPD in 1924 and founded the Socialist League.)

With approximately 400,000 members, the KPD now became, for the first time, a mass movement; under the leadership of Levi, its tactical aim was to create a united front of all proletarian parties. Only a few months later, in March 1921, the party's leadership, headed now by Heinrich Brandler and August Thalheimer, decided with the concurrence of the Communist Party of the Soviet Union that the moment had come for action. However, the so-called March Action turned into an unmistakable defeat of the KPD (particularly in Central Germany), and the party had to return to Levi's tactics which it pursued so consistently that several revolutionary opportunities, such as the murder of Rathenau, the inflation, and the Ruhr Struggle, were left essentially unexploited. As a result, there was another swing to the Left in April 1924; but since the republic was beginning to gain stability, this move had little political effect. Its ineffectiveness caused the executive committee of the Communist International (Comintern) to exert pressure, which led to the Left-wing leaders (Ruth Fischer, Arkadij Maslow) being deposed and to a new group under *Ernst (Teddy) Thälmann* (1866–1944), Heinz Neumann and Walter Ulbricht taking over the leadership of the party. Their course—concentration of forces, united-front tactics, opposition in the various parliaments and in trade unions—remained unaltered till 1929; it ran parallel to that of the Stalinist policy which sought the support of the Right in its struggle against Trotsky. When, in 1928–29 Stalin broke with the Right and initiated his policy of "building Socialism", the German party was also forced to veer to the Left (expelling the "Right", led by Brandler and Thalheimer, who founded an opposition party (KPO) in December 1928); this re-orientation was made easier by the onset of the world-wide economic crisis which followed shortly afterwards. The party was convinced that the great slump would automatically push the masses towards the Left, into the arms of the KPD, and it therefore decided to fight against the "united fascist front" in which it included the SPD.

Indeed, it directed the main force of its propaganda and political activity against the SPD, whose policies and ideology it branded "social Fascism" and whom it attacked for being a tool of the bourgeoisie against the working class and an obstacle on the road towards the dictatorship of the proletariat.

Election Results of the KPD between 1920 and 1933

Election year	Number of votes (million)	Proportion of votes in per cent	Seats
1920	0·5	2·0	4
May 1924	3·7	12·6	62
Dec. 1924	2·7	9·0	45
1928	3.2	10.6	54
1930	4.6	13.1	77
June 1932	5.3	14.6	89
Nov. 1932	5.9	16.8	100
March 1933	4.8	12.3	81

Exact membership figures are not available. It is estimated that in 1920 (after the merger with the Left wing of the USPD) the KPD had some 400,000 members; the "March Action" reduced this figure to approximately 180,000; for the year 1924 the KPD claimed a membership of between 150,000 and 180,000; for 1926—160,000; for 1931—200,000. The League of Red Front Fighters, founded in 1924, had an estimated 130,000 members (cf. Revolutionary Trade Union Opposition, discussed in the next section). The KPD's followers were by no means all unskilled workers, but came largely from the highly industrialized areas; being class bound, the KPD obviously exercised a particular attraction on workers whose self-confidence was highly developed. The organization of the KPD was at first based on cadres, which in turn rested on a system of street cells. When this system failed to achieve the desired results, the KPD changed to a system of cells in factories, where direct conflict promised a greater chance of success.

The KPD's politics became increasingly dependent on those of the Comintern, more particularly on the Communist Party of the Soviet Union; this dependence caused the party constantly to change course between tactics aimed at revolution and coups, and those of a loyal opposition. As subordination to Moscow grew, so the once extensive inter-party democracy declined to be superseded by increasingly rigid ideological dogmatism.

3. The Free Trade Unions after 1918

In November 1918, the Free Trade Unions were among those who used their influence to bring about an early return of peace and order. At first they were not primarily concerned that the new state should assume the form of a democratic republic; their growing success within the framework of the old authoritarian monarchy seemed to indicate that as long as they were given scope for their work, they could function under any system of government. While they did not militantly strive to achieve the new system, they accepted its existence and, regarding it as a pre-condition for further activity, they defended it against their own extreme Left wing. From the very beginning the leaders of the trade unions were ready and willing to play their part in tackling the new political issues: trade-union officials made up nearly a third of the Majority Socialists in the National Assembly (five of them were members of the General Committee of the Free Trade Unions, and nine were heads of individual unions); they occupied several ministerial posts (Robert Schmidt, Alexander Schlicke, Rudolf Wissell); Gustav Bauer, a member of the General Committee, headed the government in 1919–20.

The fact that trade-union leaders now shared the responsibilities of government—added to the after effects of the war—brought with it an extraordinary weakening of the trade-union organizations; a relatively untrained generation of leaders was called upon to deal with the great influx of members which followed upon the events of November 1918; large numbers had to be enrolled, organized and inspired with the tenets of trade unionism; the new leaders were not always equal to these tasks. There is no doubt that the organizational weaknesses hampered the activities of the trade-union leaders in 1918–19; but they were not the only reason why, in 1918–19, they did nothing to promote a social democracy with the means offered by the political democracy;

or why they stuck to their old, well-tried political ideas and endeavoured to stifle all utopian aspiration among their followers. Like the leaders of the SPD, they lacked a clear conception of what a social democracy is or should be.

> "We cannot solve our economic problems alone, without the employers", said Adolf Cohen, the leader of one of the largest unions, the Union of Metal Workers, when he spoke at the Trade Union Congress at Nuremberg in 1920, ". . . that would lead to exactly the same state of affairs as in Russia . . . nothing would cause us greater embarrassment than if the others were to say today : 'Here, it is all yours; get on with it !' "

The trade unions felt that their main task was to let the workers gradually accustom themselves to a planned, socialist economy, to train them to take over their proper functions within such an economic system, and to use the tools of every-day trade unionism within the framework of democratic institutions so as to speed the day when Socialism became a reality. (The Trade Union Congress of 1919 stated that "the most important preparatory task for the establishment of Socialism is assigned to the socialization of education".) In the period before the war trade-union efforts to tackle these tasks were hampered not only by the authoritarian, monarchic class system, but by the radical official party ideology. When it was decided to give the works councils a legal basis, the trade union leaders consented only after considerable hesitation, though this measure was the only concrete step towards the democratization of the economy after the workers' councils had been curbed. They feared that the works councils would take over some of the essential tasks of the trade unions; they also thought that internal, shop-floor responsibilities would distract the workers from the more general aims of the trade-union movement, and thus affect the independence of the trade unions. In the event, all these fears proved groundless.

In March 1920, a general strike called by the Free Trade Unions and the two socialist parties, and subsequently supported by the Hirsch Duncker Associations and the Christian Trade Unions, saved the republic after the army had refused to protect the government against the *putsch* led

by Dr. Kapp. During the monarchy the trade unions had
rejected strikes for political objectives; they had feared that
such actions would threaten the existence of their organizations and jeopardize their hard-won successes : in the past, a
political mass strike would have been directed against the
legal government of the country. But in 1920 the object of
the strike was to protect the republic and to defend the constitutional system of parliamentary government. By defending
the republic, the trade unions were also defending their social
achievements against an opponent who represented "the
reactionary forces of the old days". But the trade unions
wanted to do more than perpetuate the status quo, i.e. the
new republic; they wanted to make it genuinely democratic.
Their demands were subsumed under nine headings :

1. A decisive voice in the reorganization of the central and
Länder governments, and in the reform of economic and
social legislation; 2. Punishment of the participants of the
putsch; 3. Resignation of the Minister of Defence, Noske, and
of the Prussian Minister of the Interior, Heine; 4. A thorough
purge of all reactionaries in public administration and management; 5. Speedy democratization of the administration, so as
to give a decisive voice to the economic organizations of
manual and non-manual workers and civil servants; 6. Extension of existing social legislation and the immediate introduction of new legislation; 7. Immediate socialization of the
mining and electrical industries; the government to take over
the coal and potash monopolies; 8. Legal expropriation of
large landowners who fail to deliver foodstuffs or do not
cultivate their land intensively; 9. Dissolution of all counter-
revolutionary, para-military formations; organized labour to
take over security services.

The trade-union leaders were unable to put a Labour government (which was to have included all sections of the trade
unions and the two socialist parties) into power; nor were
they able to persuade a majority in parliament to include
their demands in its programme. Karl Legien and other distinguished trade unionists were unwilling to take over the
office of Reich Chancellor : they feared that if they then
failed to form a government, the whole labour movement
would swing further to the Left, away from parliamentary

democracy and towards a Soviet dictatorship. And this was exactly what they wished to prevent. It seems as if the trade unions, having put their demands to the existing state, had exhausted their strength; on their own later admission, they possessed neither the external power to enforce their demands, nor a clear conception of the political and social system into which these demands were to be embedded.

Thus, once again, the social sphere remained the main area of trade-union activity and influence; till 1924 this work was inhibited by organizational and financial weakness, due to decreased membership and the effects of inflation.

During the period of stabilization the trade unions were able to rebuild their organizations.

Membership figures for 1913–1931

Year	Members (million)	Year	Members (million)
1913	2.5	1926	3.9
1918	2.8	1928	4.9
1919	7.3	1929	4.9
1922	7.8	1930	4.7
1924	4.0	1931	4.1
1925	4.2		

In 1919 the Free Trade Unions reconstituted themselves in the General Confederation of German Trade Unions (*Allgemeiner Deutscher Gewerkschaftsbund*—ADGB), a more tightly knit organization than the former General Committee. After the death of Legien in 1920, *Theodor Leipart* (1867–1947) became the chairman of this new body. The principle of organizing unions according to industry was not always adhered to in spite of formal resolutions to this effect. The salaried employees and the civil servants had their own central organizations; the one for the salaried employees had some 462,000 members in 1930. The trade unions showed the same tendency towards a consolidation of the bureaucratic apparatus as did the SPD; the results were similar: lack of flexibility, predominance of the older age groups and an increasing alienation of members from the paid, full-time officials.

During the Weimar Republic, common interests and mutual dependence further strengthened the ties between the SPD and the Free Trade Unions: of the 156 members of the SPD in the Reich Parliament in 1928–30 56 (37 per cent) were (or rather had been before taking their seats) full-time trade union officials; the parliamentary party also included six politicians whose interests lay in the field of social welfare but who did not belong to unions. Before the First World War the SPD claimed the right to lay down policy for all labour organizations; in the Weimar Republic, however, it was the trade unions who tried to secure acceptance of their ideas by the SPD.

Confronted by the growing antagonism between workers and employers which became manifest after 1923, and with the internal political problems in the republic, the trade-union leaders came to recognize that political democracy had not brought in its wake the hoped-for democratization of social and economic life. They were as much aware of the disappointment among their own rank and file with the meagre fruits of the revolution, as of their members' "resigned flight into dreams of the future and utopias". For this reason various attempts were made after 1925 to give the concept of economic democracy—hitherto no more than a slogan with a revolutionary connotation—a concrete content and a secure theoretical foundation: "The trade-union movement does not need a distant sun but rather a goal which can be realized on earth", said *Fritz Tarnow* (1880–1951), Chairman of the Woodworkers' Union and a leading figure in the ADGB, when, in 1925, he addressed the Trade Union Congress at Breslau. The unions had to find a practicable and promising way to introduce democracy into the economy by means of the traditional methods of trade-union reformism; their objective was to hasten "the democratization of the economy as a process of transforming the capitalist into a socialist economy", and thereby to accelerate the "realization of Socialism". While the SPD remained firmly wedded to its traditional radical ideology, the trade unions continued to uphold the traditionally revisionist idea of "Socialism through democracy".

Primarily, economic democracy was to mean an advance in social policy, namely the extension of co-determination in industry, the introduction of regional organs of self-government, the promotion of public corporations, of co-operatives and of "trade-union capitalism". The theoretical discussion about economic democracy—a subject fraught with controversy within the movement itself—had no practical consequences; social security was and remained the one crucial sphere of union activity where tangible results could be achieved. In 1930 the fight for a system of unemployment insurance became for the SPD and the trade unions—under pressure from the opposition within their respective ranks— a battle in the class struggle. A compromise would have meant a betrayal of the working class affecting the unity of the labour movement and thus impairing its striking power. This was an understandable reaction to the mood of the workers whose livelihood was threatened by the world-wide slump, and to the aggressive stance of the employers: but the break up of the Grand Coalition of 1928 meant the surrender of the last possible basis for parliamentary democracy and ultimately the surrender of the republic whose survival was a necessary condition for a militantly active labour movement.

From the very beginning there was a strong radical opposition inside the ADGB against the reformist policies of the trade-union leadership, particularly from the Metal Workers' Union, in which the Revolutionary Shop Stewards were active. After 1920, the KPD sought to gain political influence among the unions who responded by expelling communist leaders and eliminating the influence of communist members by organizational devices. The constant struggle against the Communists militated against the growth of a constructive opposition inside the trade unions, where such an opposition was badly needed to redress the balance against bureaucratic tendencies and the growing isolation of the leadership. In 1928 the KPD began to form its own unions, the so-called Revolutionary Trade Union Opposition; in 1931 lack of success in this direction led to a resumption of the KPD's old tactics inside the trade unions.

CHAPTER VII

1930–1945

1. *The German Labour Movement during the Final Phase of the Republic*

When, in the general election of September 1930, the National Socialist German Workers' Party (*Nationalsozialistische Deutsche Arbeiterpartei*—NSDAP) won 107 seats and thus became the second strongest parliamentary party, it became obvious for the first time that a totalitarian party like the NSDAP, or the KPD, could destroy the system of parliamentary democracy and replace it by a dictatorship. The SPD felt that it had to tolerate the government which, led by *Heinrich Brüning* (b. 1885), stood for a constitutionally authoritarian presidential system; in order to keep the republic in existence, the party supported or at least passively submitted to measures which ran counter to its own principles or were inconsistent with the spirit of a parliamentary, democratic system; such measures were felt to be a lesser evil than a dictatorship of the Right or the Left.

After the break-up of the Grand Coalition in March 1930, the SPD went into opposition conducted along the lines of the pre-war pattern. It was without doubt to the party's advantage not to have a Minister in the "Cabinet of social reaction"; it also gave it a better chance of dealing with the rivalry of of the KPD, with the general fragmentation of the Left (in 1933 there were some 20 socialist groups, including the two major parties), and with Left-wing pressures inside the party itself. But, on the debit side, it meant giving up the chance of translating the social force of the working class into political power. Though Brüning's deflationary policy was by no means uncontroversial, neither the SPD nor the trade unions could offer a viable alternative to halt the slump.

This passive, almost helpless reaction to the world-wide

economic crisis and to the threat to the republic revealed once again the fatal inertia which had so often overtaken the SPD's militant, originally revolutionary impetus. Having abandoned an exact analysis of the forces in society, the party was unable to reach conclusions on political action. Moreover, it misread the increasingly revolutionary situation among the workers. There was also a hidden fear of taking over political power.

When, in July 1932, Papen was poised to strike at Prussia, the SPD displayed the same mixture of political perplexity and passivity on the one hand, and of a readiness for sacrifice and a sense of responsibility on the other; the party executive declared that "come what may, we shall not abandon the legal basis of the Constitution". Its only protest took the form of court proceedings : the social-democratic Prime Minister of Prussia, Otto Braun, brought a case before the Supreme (Constitutional) Court. Beyond this, the party leaders merely consoled themselves and their followers with the prospect of an early general election, when, ballot-paper in hand, the power of the labour organizations could be proved; one would not, so they agreed, let one's opponent dictate one's actions. The decline of the NSDAP vote in November 1932 (accompanied by the very first signs of improvement in world trade) was interpreted as a sign that sanity was returning to the political scene and would save the democratic system. Behind these arguments there lay a dislike of extra-parliamentary action and of the incalculable risks involved; a fear of causing bloodshed; the rigid adherence to parliamentary forms of struggle in which all political thought was frozen; and possibly also a secret fear of the consequences of an improbable victory.

In his book "Von Weimar bis Hitler" (1940), Otto Braun maintains that a republican uprising in July 1932 would have amounted to criminal folly in view of the heavily armed Reichswehr, the militant reactionary bands, and the conceivably ambivalent attitude of the Prussian police (pp. 256–7). The trade union leaders felt that a general strike was not feasible at that particular time. Yet Wilhelm Hoegner, M.P. from Bavaria, wrote in 1920 in his memoirs "Der schwierige Aussenseiter" that resistance then might have spared the

German people the sacrifices of the war later. It is impossible
to decide in retrospect who was right. Goebbels, however,
wrote in his diary on 21 July 1932 : "The Reds have missed
their great hour. It will never return."

The attitude of the SPD leaders after 1930 was the subject
of violent controversy within the party. In 1931 the Left split
away and, led by Max Seydewitz, Kurt Rosenfeld and Ernst
Eckstein, founded the SAP; this was a final attempt to create
the pre-conditions for a unified revolutionary organization "of
the socialist labour movement on a national and international
foundation" (Statement of Principles of the SAP, 1932). But
at this late stage the SAP was unable to arouse among the
workers the hoped-for response for a fight against Fascism.
The "New Right", which included mainly the younger
generation of leaders (*Carlo Mierendorff*, 1897–1943; *Julius
Leber*, 1891–1945; *Theodor Haubach*, 1896–1945; *Kurt
Schumacher*, 1895–1952), was similarly unable to make its
point of view prevail in the party. These young politicians
saw that the SPD was losing its hold on the German labour
movement, and recognized the danger to the republic which
this implied; they insisted therefore, that the party must
become a power outside parliament, as it had once been inside
it; that it must, beyond its present negative posture, seize the
initiative by setting itself positive goals; it must try to instill
in the workers an emotional commitment to the socialist vision
of state, economy and society. The leaders of the party saw
in these proposals nothing more than an unjustified attempt
to throw overboard their well-tried political ideology and
tactics; or they regarded them as an expression of unbridled
political ambition or as youthful impatience.

In support of their arguments against the "young", the
party leaders adduced the faithfulness and discipline of their
followers; in this assumption they were not altogether justified.
After 1930 the number of votes cast for the SPD diminished
both absolutely and relatively. Though an analysis of the
election figures shows that the total vote for all parties of the
Left remained more or less constant, one cannot overlook the
fact that after 1930 a number of younger working-class voters
switched their allegiance to the Right, to the NSDAP.
Basically, German labour remained faithful to its traditional

convictions; yet within the socialist camp there was an upsurge of radicalism which favoured the KPD and enabled it, in the last phase of the republic, to overtake the SPD by a wide margin in certain electoral districts.

The SPD and KPD together achieved the following election results : 1930 13.1 million votes, 37.6 per cent; July 1932 : 13.2 million votes, 36.2 per cent; November 1932 : 13.3 million votes, 37.2 per cent. In 1930–32 the KPD gained more votes than the SPD in five electoral districts : Berlin, Merseburg, Cologne-Aachen, East Dusseldorf and West Dusseldorf.

The KPD's gains derived mainly from among the ranks of unorganized workers whose wretchedness (February 1932 : 6.12 million unemployed, including 44.9 per cent of the total trade-union membership) made them despair of the political methods of the SPD and of the republic generally. But the attitude of the organized workers was also very ambivalent : there was much doubt about the policies of the SPD which seemed to many to lack the radicalism necessary to avert the menace of National Socialism. Many workers wondered whether it was in fact worth while to stand up for the Weimar Republic which appeared to them once again as a state dominated by "the others". The resulting passivity and list-lessness could often be overcome by recourse to traditional, pseudo-revolutionary theory : the social and political developments which threatened the existence of the workers were interpreted as the long anticipated end of capitalism, an end which heralded a new beginning and inaugurated the victory of the working class. The menace of National Socialism after 1930 also loosed "a stirring wave of militant impulses which deeply agitated the humdrum party existence" and contrasted sharply with the party's "depressing impotence" (Matthias, "Die Sozialdemokratie", p. 84). This militant potential was never put to the test, because the party leaders never gave the signal for an attack; long established party discipline prevented spontaneous action even among those who were ready to fight.

After the Papen coup against Prussia on 20 July 1932, the party leadership continued along established paths; in spite of the personal courage of individual leaders, they pursued a policy of "quiescence". Even after 30 January 1933 the party leaders were prepared, in order to keep the party in existence, to steer a course adapted to the changed circumstances, insofar as this could be reconciled with the party's dignity and its old principles. There was talk of the inevitability of economic development which must lead to the victory of the working class; the policy based on the slogan: "Our foes will perish through our legality", which had been so successful against Bismarck, was quoted as a precedent and regarded as applicable to the fight against Hitler. The legalistic attitude prevalent among the party's top echelons finally induced them to attempt an opportunist accommodation to the national-socialist régime; thus, e.g., on 30 March 1933 the SPD left the Labour and Socialist International; on 17 May 1933 the remnants of the SPD's parliamentary party, led by the former *Reichstag* President *Paul Löbe* (1875–1967), consented—admittedly under threat of murder by the national-socialist Minister of the Interior Frick—to support the government's declaration on foreign policy (a step which was not approved by those members of the executive who had already gone into exile). But all this was of no avail. On 22 June 1933 the SPD was proscribed, its organizations were smashed, its followers persecuted, arrested and forced to emigrate—deeply hurt, but not without hope. On 23 March the SPD had been the only party which, consistently exploiting the parliamentary possibilities left to it, refused to pass the Enabling Bill; in a courageous speech the leader of the party *Otto Wels* (1873–1939) declared, *inter alia*:

It is idle to try to turn back the wheel of history... In this historical hour, we, the German Social Democrats, solemnly pledge ourselves to uphold the principles of humanity and justice, of freedom and Socialism. No Enabling Act will give you (the Government) the power to destroy ideas which are perennial and indestructible...

While we cannot but admire the courage behind these almost prophetic words, they cannot conceal the fact that the SPD, though bitterly opposing National Socialism, failed clearly to recognize its totalitarian and revolutionary character. The crucial reason for this failure was the party's

adherence to certain conceptual frameworks which dated
from the period before the war. These included :

1. The prejudice in favour of traditional, allegedly proved
fighting methods which confined the SPD's struggle within
the limits of parliamentary action and constitutional legality;
as a consequence of this legalistic thinking, they opposed
National Socialism with weapons which were not equal to
that party's totalitarian nature.

2. An almost limitless organizational patriotism which endowed the organizations of the labour movement with a myth
of indestructibility, raised their perpetuation to an end in
itself, and, in the final analysis, did not exclude opportunist
rapprochement to the national-socialist régime.

3. The ideological inflexibility which found its main expression in the belief in an economically predetermined development with its promise of the victory of the working class, and
in the refusal to analyse the actually prevailing conditions of
society; the staleness of the SPD's programme in the Weimar
Republic helped to drive salaried workers, the urban middle
class and the farmers towards National Socialism; the SPD
(as well as the KPD) was the party which had predicted that
the victory of capitalism would bring with it the progressive
pauperization of the middle strata; it therefore had to bear
the brunt of the resentment of those sections of the population whose livelihood was now actually threatened.

4. The assumption that men, both individually and together,
were imbued by ideas of enlightenment and by political
humanism. This view overestimated man by regarding him as
on the whole good and reasonable; it overlooked the dangerous
attraction of irrational political forces, and lost the capacity
to recognize and combat them.

None of the other democratic parties offered a more effective way of combating National Socialism than the SPD; on
the contrary, the democratic substance of these organizations
waned visibly towards the end of the republic; finally the
Social Democrats became "the last defenders of the written
Constitution and of the long abandoned parliamentary
system" (Matthias, *"Die Sozialdemokratie"*, p. 90).

The KPD itself had declared that the German people
could only choose between Communism and National
Socialism; as a result of this the lower-middle as well as the

upper-middle class and conservative and ecclesiastical circles let themselves be persuaded that a national-socialist victory would save Germany from Bolshevism. It is an open question whether the KPD could ever have achieved its political objective of seizing power: the highest proportion of votes which it ever secured was in November 1932, when it polled 16·8 per cent. Towards the end of the Weimar Republic the KPD finally recognized the extent to which its own existence was threatened; it therefore tried to revise its anti-SPD policies and to create a "united working class front". But by then the SPD's deep and justified suspicions of the KPD prevented the realization of such plans; it was too late to do anything— and the KPD became the first victim of the national-socialist reign of terror.

The executive of the ADGB largely shared the views held by the SPD leaders during the final phase of the Weimar Republic; the two organizations to a great extent supported and confirmed each other's arguments. It was not till the so-called Schleicher Experiment was mooted that some basic differences between the SPD leaders and the trade unions emerged: in December 1932–January 1933 the trade unions were not averse to the creation of a "trade union axis" to support Schleicher's authoritarian presidential government against the NSDAP; the party rejected this plan. The project itself presages the political opportunism of the trade-union leaders which, after 30 January 1933, found expression in relation to the national-socialist régime.

The trade-union leaders, like so many others, failed to recognize the full extent of the national-socialist menace; they held fast to the principle of legality. "Organization—not demonstration" was their watchword. They hoped that by increasingly adapting themselves to the new régime, they could keep the trade-union organizations intact (possibly as seed beds of future resistance). In the end they succumbed to the illusion that there must be scope for peaceful means of opposing even the National Socialists.

On 20 March 1933 the central executive of the ADGB stated *inter alia* that the social tasks of the unions must be fulfilled irrespective of "the prevailing form of government"; on 21 March a written declaration to this effect was handed to

Hitler by the Chairman of the ADGB, Leipart. On 29 March Hitler received a second letter from Leipart which informed him that the trade unions had severed their connections with the SPD. On 15 April the ADGB welcomed the announcement that the First of May would henceforth be a national holiday, and gave permission to its members to take part in the celebrations; on 19 April the statement was altered and now recommended that members participate in the festivities. On 22 April there followed the rupture between the ADGB and the International Confederation of Labour; on 30 April the General Free Association of Salaried Employees (*Allgemeiner Freier Angestellten-Bund*—AFA-Bund) was dissolved. On 1 May only a small number of trade unionists took part in the official celebrations organized by the National Socialists; on 2 May all trade-union buildings throughout Germany were occupied, trade-union funds confiscated and trade-union leaders taken into "protective custody".

All that has been said earlier about the SPD applies *a fortiori* to the Free Trade Unions : they failed, because they tried to keep their organizations alive by the desperate gambit of committing political suicide.

In the middle of April 1933, shortly before the trade-union movement was destroyed, pressure of circumstances made the trade-union leaders of all shades of opinion propose the formation of a unified movement; but it was too late to translate this idea into reality. Even if the circumstances had been different, it is debatable whether the time was ripe for genuine unity. It was not till the leading trade unionists of all sections (Leuschner, Kaiser, Habermann) joined ranks in common opposition to National Socialism that a basis of trust was established upon which the concept of a unified trade union could be developed.

2. *National Socialism and Labour in the "Third Reich"*

Belying its pretentious name, the National Socialist German Workers' Party was never—neither before nor after 1933— a workers' party, let alone a socialist party: in 1930 the proportion of manual workers in the NSDAP was 28.1 per cent (manual workers constituted 45.9 per cent of all persons employed in industry and trade); in 1935 this figure rose to 32.2 per cent (and 46.3 per cent respectively).

In its 1920 programme the NSDAP promised "the abolition of all unearned income" (point 11), "complete confiscation of war profits" (12), "nationalization of all joint stock holding companies (trusts)" (13), "profit-sharing in large concerns" (14), "an immediate take-over of large stores into municipal ownership, to be then let at low rentals to small traders" (16), "a land reform corresponding to our national needs; legislation to expropriate without compensation land required for communal purposes" (17).

Not a single point of this programme was ever translated into practice in the "Third Reich"; indeed, at the instigation of pressure groups, point 17 was amended as early as 1928; the new version stated that the NSDAP is "based on private property". After 1933 the emergence of the Nazi party officials admittedly caused a shift in the ruling strata of society; it is also true that the economy was ultimately under complete state control; but the underlying capitalist economic and social structure remained virtually untouched. The real state of affairs was glossed over by ideological slogans about "national union", "Germans, creating by the labour of brow and fist" (*sic, "die schaffenden Deutschen der Stirn und Faust"*), etc.

Nor was the "Socialism" of the NSDAP anything but a means to a political end; Hitler regarded the "masses" of workers as a convenient tool of his militant movement; in *"Mein Kampf"* he openly admits that he had the model of the marxist labour movement in mind, with its obvious skill of swaying the masses. He had no understanding or sympathy for the marxist movement's humanitarian goal, the emancipation of the oppressed; yet the strength of the labour movement derived from this goal and not, as Hitler believed, from propagandist tricks. Hitler's contempt for human beings, and particularly for the workers, is illustrated by his frequent derogatory reference to the "mass".

The initially strong socialist wing of the NSDAP, led by Georg Strasser, with Gottfried Feder and Count Reventlow as its ideological spokesmen, could not prevail against Hitler, who had formerly been called "the little bourgeois". After

1933 it soon became obvious what Hitler's "Socialism" really meant : it was intended to relate exclusively to the state and to serve as a means of making Germany internally and externally strong in preparation for the coming war. Robert Ley revealed the core of national "Socialism" with his usual primitive candour :

> What is good for Germany, that is right; what harms Germany, that is wrong. Thus Socialism is not, in the final analysis, the concern for and the welfare of the individual, but the question : What is good for Germany? What is good for this nation?

The Left wing of the NSDAP recognized the trade unions in principle, but demanded that they become apolitical so that they might be used as a tool for the party's own ends. Hitler seems to have been prepared to tolerate the trade unions prior to 1933 for the same reasons. At that time he had no intention of forming national-socialist trade unions; such unions would sooner or later have become involved in social and political disputes with the employers; and the NSDAP had to avoid any conflict with the employers who played an indispensable part in the party's rise to power.

The first blow against the German labour movement after the National Socialists came to power was struck as early as April 1933, when the "Law relating to Industrial Representation . . ." was passed; according to it the authorities could depose works council members whose "attitude was antagonistic to the government or the economy", and nominate members of the NSDAP to the councils. The law was the régime's reaction to the works council elections of March 1933, when, in spite of propaganda and pressure, the NSDAP gained only 25 per cent of the votes. Before they smashed the trade unions in May 1933, the National Socialists engineered their psychologically shrewdest deception: on 10 April 1933 a law was passed making the First of May, the day which had since 1899 been consecrated to the struggle of the international labour movement, a public holiday, a "Day of National Labour". The National Socialists, particularly Ley, justified the dissolution of the trade unions by the struggle against Bolshevism and by alleged instances of corruption; both these "justifications" were again cleverly designed to appeal to the mentality of the German people.

As a substitute for trade unions, a mammoth organization, the German Labour Front (*Deutsche Arbeitsfront*—DAF), was created under the aegis of Robert Ley; in its early days it had a pseudo-democratic structure and retained the services of minor officials of the former trade unions. This, as much as the choice of name, was designed to convince the German worker that the NSDAP had no other aim in view than a united trade-union front, i.e. an objective which had always been considered desirable.

But the DAF was in reality nothing but an organization for national-socialist indoctrination and propaganda aimed at the German workers (of whom 10 per cent eluded obligatory membership till the end of the "Third Reich"). The very high income from members' subscriptions (in 1939 it had 30 million members who had to contribute 1.5 per cent of their wage or salary), and the sequestrated trade-union funds made the DAF one of the wealthiest of the party's organizations; but it could not influence the economy. Towards the end of 1933 the organization Strength through Joy (*Kraft durch Freude*) was constituted within the DAF; this grew into a giant leisure industry (with 150,000 officials), whose disguised social object was the care and orientation of the workers in the interest of the totalitarian state.

The National Socialists had good reasons for leaving intact the social benefits which the German labour movement had won before 1933; but they destroyed every vestige of demo-cratic independence and self-government. The law of 19 May 1933 abolished collective agreements and independent (and, in exceptional cases, government) arbitration; Hitler appointed thirteen "labour trustees" for the whole of Germany; they were officials of the Ministry of Labour and laid down wage scales and conditions of work on behalf of the state. "The Law for the Regulation of National Labour", enacted on 20 January 1934, introduced the leadership principle into the inner structure of industrial and commercial concerns.

Even before the outbreak of war, the national-socialist régime abolished the workers' freedom to choose their place of employment (1938—introduction of direction of labour): the workers were soldiers in the service of the régime. The new terminology for describing their surroundings bore the stamp of this military conception: "labour action", "work battles", "factory roll-calls", "serving the Führer and the nation", and similar expressions entered everyday speech. Under the national-socialist régime the entrepreneurs, the urban middle class and the farmers considerably increased their material security and social prestige; the organization of the economy on corporate lines even brought them a measure of recognized representation similar to that of professional organizations. The workers on the other hand were the only section of the population which was not directly represented: they were "looked after" and kept dependent like members of an army; nor did their material conditions appreciably change. Though Germany, parallel to the rest of the world, surmounted the worst of the slump and by 1936 already achieved full employment—mainly as a result of re-armament—the National Socialists had pegged wages, first by indirect methods and, after 1939, by direct ones: wages rose but little above their low 1932–3 levels. Though full employment, the end of the short working week and the employment of dependants raised the standard of living of the working population, it never again reached the high levels of 1928–30.

Thanks to full employment, the continuance of state welfare policies, slogans designed to appeal to the mentality of the workers, and, last but not least, the growing reign of terror, the National Socialists gradually managed to overcome the negative attitude of the workers; nevertheless, the German labour movement's contribution to the resistance against Hitler was relatively greater than that of any other section of the community.

3. The Resistance from the Ranks of the Labour Movement

After 30 January 1933 the National Socialists completed the seizure of power and consolidated it behind a façade of fierce nationalist propaganda and of pseudo-legal measures such as the Enabling Act. The political opponents of the régime were eliminated by open terror and violence; they were arrested, ill-treated, murdered, forced to emigrate or to go underground.

After the SPD had been declared illegal on 22 June 1933, a new wave of terror set in, during which among others Schumacher was arrested on 6 July 1933; he was detained in various prisons and concentration camps till March 1943; he was in custody again from September 1943 till February 1944, and again in August–September 1944. The KPD leader Ernst Thälmann was arrested after the Reichstag fire on 3 March 1933; after eleven years of imprisonment, he was murdered in the Buchenwald concentration camp in August 1944.

Though the labour organizations were in ruins and the majority of their leaders either in custody or in enforced exile, organized resistance against the régime existed from the very beginning. It was not centrally organized, but consisted at first of usually small local groups which met under the guise of debating clubs, reading circles, sports clubs, etc. The leaders of these groups came mainly from the labour youth movement, from the *Reichsbanner* and from the ranks of social-democratic students; most of them were former Radicals from the Left or the Right wing of the SPD. These resistance groups were thus not representative of the old party; the legalistic outlook of the party's leaders had in no way prepared its members for illegal activities. Many of the older Social Democrats, though consistently opposed to the régime, could not be expected to take an active part in the resistance movement for social reasons, e.g. because of their family responsibilities. Several resistance groups were able to build up geographically ramified organizations, e.g. the *Rote Stosstrupp* (Red Shock Troops), an association of students and young workers in Berlin; a group of revolutionary Socialists (members of the Left wing of the SAJ and former Communists) who called themselves *Neu Beginnen* had combined as early as 1931 so as to be ready to oppose Hitler's anticipated seizure of power. (One of its members was *Fritz Erler* (1913–1967), who was arrested in 1938 and sentenced to ten years hard labour in 1939.) Socialist groups, such as the ISK and the SAP, who had stood outside the SPD before 1933, proved themselves far better prepared for illegal activities: ideology, discipline and organization on the principle of individual cells made these numerically small groups extremely effective. Their achievements in the underground resistance were considerable;

of particular interest here is the successful collaboration of the resistance organizations inside Germany with their counterparts in exile. The KPD and its splinter groups—the KPO and the Trotskyites—offered centrally organized resistance from the very beginning; in terms of human lives, the KPD in particular paid a very high price for this resistance.

Most groups (with the exception of the ISK and the SAP) were convinced that the Hitler régime would not last long; accordingly they concentrated their illegal activities on keeping alive democratic ideas and on preparing immediate operations:

> they printed and distributed leaflets, newspapers, journals and pamphlets which were either prepared in Germany or infiltrated from abroad; they encouraged attitudes hostile to National Socialism, particularly in large concerns; occasionally, as at the Olympic Games, they made attempts to influence public opinion on a large scale. They arranged hiding places for the persecuted, gave help towards emigration and cared for the families of the régime's victims; in some cases they even managed to free detainees.

Hitler's successes at home and abroad led to a consolidation of the régime, which lasted till 1936; many of his former opponents came to terms with the "Third Reich"—blinded by its success or cowed by the Gestapo terror; by 1936–38 the Gestapo had also managed to smash the majority of the workers' resistance centres. Under these conditions resistance could amount to little more than keeping alive and consolidating political convictions inimical to the régime, and preparing members of the underground for the period after Hitler's defeat. The resistance groups which were held together by common political or religious convictions, and to an even greater extent the many individuals who were driven into opposition by feelings of human decency had to muster a prodigious amount of mental fortitude; among hostile surroundings, in the midst of a nation increasingly addicted to the existing régime, these groups and individuals freely chose self-imposed isolation.

At the outbreak of war some 300,000 Germans were in concentration camps for political offences. This figure is given by

Weisenborn, who adds : "We may assume with certainty that up to 1939 the majority of political detainees belonged to the labour movement" (p. 149). Of the 1,807 political prisoners executed in the Brandenburg prison between 1940 and 1945, 773 were manual workers and artisans, 363 salaried employees and civil servants (cf. Weisenborn, p. 258). A report sent by social-democratic officials to the SPD executive in exile in 1936 contains the following information about the attitude of the workers to National Socialism (quoted in Leber/Moltke : "*Für und wider*", p. 181): "Bavarian Motor Works (BMW), Munich : ... Though they must all yield to the prevailing pressure, they show, whenever possible, that they are not very interested in all the Hitler twaddle. This emerged again clearly when the Führer's last speech was broadcast to the assembled workers ... Attendance was obligatory. During the speech the workers talked among themselves so much that the factory Storm Troopers had to intervene to restore some sort of order ... At one point during the last third of the speech there was lengthy applause on the wireless. The workers immediately rushed to the exits, demanding to be let out because the speech was over. The guards at the doors were taken by surprise and there followed a general exodus. Indeed, windows were opened and men pushed through them as if they were fleeing ..."

The Second World War, unleashed by the National Socialists and predicted by the German labour movement even before 1933, gave a new impetus to the resistance movement. The guiding lines of the social-democratic resistance were laid down by the younger party leaders who had been released from custody after the régime had firmly established itself : *Wilhelm Leuschner* (1890–1944), Minister of the Interior of Hesse between 1928 and 1933, and Deputy Chairman of the ADGB in 1932, was instrumental in setting up a secret trade-union resistance organization; together with *Jakob Kaiser* (1888–1961) of the Christian Trade Unions and Max Habermann of the German National Shop Assistants' Union, he worked out an ideological basis for the unified trade unions of the future, and sought to determine the position of labour in a free society; (these efforts enjoyed the support of the historian Ludwig Reichhold and Dr. Elfriede Negben); the three men took a leading part in the preparations for the events of 20 July. (The proposed government was to have been headed by Goerdeler, with Leuschner as Vice-Chancellor.) Both Carlo Mierendorff and Theodor Haubach could have gone abroad after being released from concentration camps, but preferred to remain in Germany to rebuild socialist resistance; both men were members of Count Moltke's Kreisau circle. Julius Leber worked along similar lines; he was in close touch with Mierendorff, Haubach and Leuschner, and had the support of Gustav Dahrendorf and Adolf Reichwein; he was also a close personal friend of Stauffenberg, and was to have been Minister of the Interior after the plot of 20 July.

The catholic labour movement also intensified its resistance activities during the war; its main protagonists were Nikolaus Gross, Dr. Otto Müller, Dr. H. J. Schmitt and Bernhard Letterhaus.

> After 20 July Leuschner, Leber, Haubach, Reichwein, Letterhaus and Gross were executed (Mierendorff died during an air attack on Leipzig in 1943); Dr. Otto Müller died in prison at the age of seventy-four, as a result of ill-treatment; Habermann committed suicide so as not to betray the other participants of the plot; Körner, who died after being liberated in 1945, Dahrendorf and H. J. Schmitt were sentenced to long terms of hard labour; Jakob Kaiser managed to stay in hiding near Berlin till the end of the war; Joseph Joos had been in custody since 1940.

The Communists too rebuilt their resistance groups during the war: the members of the *Rote Kapelle,* led by Harro Schultze-Boysen and Arvid Harnack, were mainly young (not only communist) intellectuals; they maintained contact with socialist groups in the West and in the Soviet Union (in 1941–42 by wireless); the leaders of this group were executed in 1942. Another important communist resistance group collected around Anton Saefkow, Franz Jacob and Bernhard Bästlein; in 1943–44 they built up, from Berlin, an efficient and widely ramified organization among workers opposed to the régime; they also kept in touch with social-democrat and bourgeois resistance circles; in 1944 the group was betrayed by an informer; Saefkow and numerous others were arrested by the Gestapo and executed.

Finally we must mention the resistance of many minor

groups and individuals; so far little or nothing is known about them (even at this date no comprehensive account of the workers' resistance in the "Third Reich" is available); they helped Jews, foreign workers, prisoners of war and other victims of persecution; they listened to enemy broadcasts and disseminated the information which they had monitored, they refused to serve in the armed forces and to carry out criminal orders—all at the risk of their lives. All of them, the known and the nameless resistance fighters against National Socialism, shared the conviction of Julius Leber who, shortly before his execution on 5 January 1945, said in a message to his friends: "One's life is the proper price to pay for so righteous and just a cause".

4. The SPD in Exile

At a "national conference" on 27 April 1933, the SPD elected a new executive "in order to rejuvenate and re-activate the party"; on 4 May, after the suppression of the trade unions, the party in the Saar set up a "foreign delegacy" of six members of the executive; when, on 17 May 1933, the rest of the executive, who had remained in Berlin, agreed to the government's declaration on foreign policy, there followed a rupture between the Berlin group and the "foreign delegacy", i.e. the party's representatives abroad. The latter had moved their headquarters to Prague, where, after the dissolution of the SPD on 22 June 1933, they constituted themselves into the SPD's executive.

On 27 April 1933 the executive included *inter alia* Otto *Wels*, Chairman; *Hans Vogel* (1879–1945), Deputy Chairman; *Siegfried Aufhäuser* (b. 1884), Chairman of the AFA-Bund; *Erich Ollenhauer* (1901–1963), Chairman of the SAJ since 1928; *Friedrich Stampfer* (1874–1957), editor-in-chief of *"Vorwärts"* since 1916; *Paul Löbe* and *Wilhelm Sollmann* (1881–1951). Wels, Vogel, Stampfer and Ollenhauer were members of the foreign delegacy of the SPD; Sollmann and Aufhäuser emigrated, Löbe was in custody in 1933 and 1944. In 1937 the party executive moved its headquarters to Paris because of Hitler's pressure on the Czechoslovak government; in 1940, following the German victory against France, most SPD leaders managed to make their way illegally across Spain to Lisbon; Vogel, Ollenhauer and others went to London (Wels died in 1939); Stampfer and Sollmann fled to the United States; Rudolf Hilferding and Rudolf Breitscheid were caught by the Gestapo; Hilferding died in the Paris Gestapo prison in 1944, allegedly by his own hand; Breitscheid perished in 1944 in the Buchenwald concentration camp during an air raid.

The party's executive in exile felt that its task was to lead and organize a revolutionary movement of the SPD against National Socialism. The leaders of the legal party had by force of circumstances become revolutionaries; their practical experience of leadership and their theoretical convictions about the meaning of the workers' struggle had now to be applied to their new task. They believed that reason and the desire for freedom would prevail in Germany and that the nation, led by the labour movement, would rise against Hitler's dictatorship; they hoped that economic and external difficulties, which would eventually face the régime, could contribute to an uprising; they regarded Hitler and the "Third Reich" (at least till 1935) as transient phenomena; Hitler's downfall seemed to them inevitable. They underestimated their opponent while at the same time overestimating the strength of the resistance among the German people against National Socialism : the overwhelming majority of the people stood solidly behind Hitler. Their assessment of the importance of the German resistance movement was similarly incorrect. During the war, the German Socialists in exile were almost completely cut off from the underground movement in Germany; the events of 20 July appear to have taken them completely by surprise, in spite of the fact that social-democratic leaders had taken an active part in the plot. In spite of its remoteness and of the growing hopelessness of its struggle, the party executive was never tempted to accede to proposals by the Communists to form a united proletarian front; the full importance of this stand to the cause of democratic Socialism did not become apparent till after 1945.

The SPD in exile split into a multitude of groups, each with different ideas about the party's past, about the conduct of its affairs in exile, and about the future ideological and practical image of the party.

When the fragmentation of the social-democratic groups in exile had reached its height in 1938, a meeting took place in London, at which the rest of the party's executive in exile (Vogel, Ollenhauer), together with the group *Neu Beginnen*, the SAP and the ISK (Willi Eichler), formed the Union of German Socialist Organizations in Great Britain; this group, whose further development was influenced by indigenous Labour-Socialism, played a crucial part in the shaping of the re-constituted SPD after 1945. In New York, however, the different fractions were unable to settle their organizational and ideological differences.

In spite of all the disagreements, the debate about the basic principles of the SPD which went on both in Germany and abroad seemed gradually to yield the outline of a new party : a party which still primarily relies on the workers, but which has ceased to be a one-class party; a party which regards the nation as a prerequisite for the realization of its policies and as a leading element in a closely knit political community of the democratic nations of Europe; a party to whom the class struggle means nothing beyond a struggle to transform the life of the entire nation in a manner which would create a synthesis of freedom and social justice.

CHAPTER VIII

1945–1965

1. The Position of the Workers in Present-Day Society

It would seem that the worker of today is no longer a proletarian; his income has risen above subsistence level, his way of life and his outlook increasingly approximate to those of the middle strata whose members are traditionally described as petit bourgeois; but above all else, the worker of today lacks (militant) class consciousness.

The proletarian, propertyless and with no resources on which to fall back, is dependent on the demand for the commodity which he offers for sale, namely his labour; he cannot plan, he has no security, he is expendable, perpetually dependent and with hardly any chance of crossing the class barrier; his position, which is that of an object, shapes his consciousness. In this classical sense we can no longer describe the workers of the Federal Republic as proletarians who have nothing to lose but their chains. Their own efforts and struggles have played a crucial role in increasing their social security, raising their standard of living and thereby changing their outlook.

And yet some of the intrinsic elements of a proletarian existence are still with us, even though—being affected by the development of society in general—they may appear in a different guise. The workers' share in the material and spiritual riches of our technological civilization remains very limited: prosperity is relative, and cannot be measured by material yardsticks alone.

The worker's chances of planning his life remain circumscribed, as they have always been; the fear of unemployment still plays an important part in his assessment of his own situation; technological unemployment, brought about by automation, does in fact constitute a potential threat to his

security. The worker's subjective feeling of being expendable
and dependent not only today but for the rest of his life is
caused by concrete facts: many occupations which were
traditionally taught as crafts have lost not only their social
but also their economic value; because of rationalization and
automation, the semi-skilled worker, trained to perform a
single operation, is gaining ground compared with the highly
skilled specialist; no sooner do many apprentices acquire
the skill of their trade than they have to be retrained. Many
middle-aged workers see their occupational qualifications
devalued and many old workers find themselves at the end
of their working lives in a situation not appreciably different
from that of their early years. In some cases they may have
to give up work altogether, because they can no longer fit
in with new production methods.

The lowering of occupational prestige is not necessarily
accompanied by diminished earning power; but the question
whether that which a man achieves in his work and accom-
plishes in his life appears worth while to him and to others
is obviously more important to him than money. Today a
manual worker has few opportunities to achieve personal
satisfaction or gain recognition for his efforts (we shall have
more to say about non-manual workers later): man's self-
alienation—one of Marx's criteria of capitalist production—
continues in our day.

One factor which greatly inhibits the worker's efforts to
gain personal and social recognition is the pseudo-military
pattern on which industrial organization still tends to model
itself; however much employers may stress that good management nowadays requires that everyone should make their
contribution in thought, word and deed, the fact remains that
the worker (and employee generally) leaves his freedom in his
locker along with his overcoat. Moral as well as material ties
are necessary if an enterprise is to be run on the lines of a
quasi-monarchy; the workers must be given not only bonuses,
additional welfare provisions, retirement pensions, housing and
organized leisure facilities, but be surrounded by an atmo-
sphere of paternal goodwill, of mutual involvement and
dependence such as exist in a family.

Efforts by employers to achieve this end are extremely

significant : a sense of belonging is as important to the worker as social security. This fact should give pause to labour organizations which at the present time seem to place overmuch emphasis on the achievement of material gains; it should make them think about the real meaning of their work if they do not want to lose the battle against the employers for the workers' soul. At the same time we must keep in mind that the longing for a social refuge, unless balanced by a constant desire for independence and for social responsibility, may amount to a flight from the need to fashion one's own life.

The trend towards a modern industrial feudalism along paternalistic lines reduces the interest, never very strong, which people take in political and social issues; it encourages the idea of a society in which there are no conflicts and in which the state assumes the functions of a regulative, conciliatory superior authority; it deprives those who believe in democratic pluralism—as e.g. labour unions—of the psychological basis on which to function effectively.

It seems conceivable that automation may bring about changes in the underlying structure of industry : it may weaken (if not altogether eliminate) the hierarchic pattern of individual concerns by increasing the worker's scope for responsibility and decision-making, while at the same time increasing his isolation. In this context we may also note a gradual assimilation of the functions of manual to those of non-manual workers. While we may hope that this will overcome the deeply ingrained and unreal idea of "class" barriers, we cannot but fear that industrial concerns may become structured along the lines of the sociological pattern which applies to present day society in general : on the one hand a small group of highly qualified and privileged specialists, on the other an expendable mass of semi-skilled labour.

It is not yet possible to assess the individual and social significance of the physical and psychological effects of automation on workers. The revolutionary transformation which individuals and society are currently undergoing is best gauged by considering the list of qualities which a worker engaged in the automated production process is expected to possess : mobility, the ability to conform, a quick grasp (of phenomena which often cannot be fully understood), the ability to think abstractly, willingness to make decisions; but at the same time precision, reliability, ability to work with others and a sense of responsibility. Not only has the emphasis shifted from the worker's physical to his mental and spiritual resources, but we look in vain for the values traditionally associated with the ethics of labour, e.g. diligence, obedience and willingness. On the other hand, the above list of requirements foreshadows the terrific tension to which the "homo futurus" will be subjected. How, for example, can a man be expected to be fully adaptable and highly flexible and at the same time entirely reliable?

How do the workers see themselves and society in the circumstances which we have just outlined? The self-appraisal of the (skilled) workers exhibits two contradictory features: in respect of their occupational status and performance the workers rank themselves very high, putting themselves fourth on the scale below doctors, technicians, engineers and university professors, but above teachers, directors, foremen (9th), civil servants (13th) and other salaried employees (15th). However, when it comes to social status, the position is reversed: many workers see society divided into those "above" and those "below", and themselves as on the lowest rung of the social ladder. The "above" starts with foremen, members of works councils, trade union secretaries; salaried employees also belong to the "other side".

How is this discrepancy to be explained? Though strongly aware of their own attainments and the importance of their work, the workers have learned from experience that they have little to hope for beyond higher pay and shorter hours, that there is hardly any real prospect of their participating in the shaping of the industrial scene, even less of sharing in public responsibilities. So the barrier between "them up there" and "us down here" remains, frustrating all attempts to change the authority-based structure of our society; social conduct and attitudes are perpetuated, moulded by mistrust, doubt, pretended conformity, or by the flight from the hopelessness of everyday existence into a world of phantasy.

The salaried employee also continues to see himself as he always did: he knows about "above" and "below" and ranks himself in the middle, while at the same time developing a fine capacity for sensing and discriminating between social gradations. For him society is not divided in two, but arranged hierarchically; within the hierarchy he sees the possibility of eventual advancement. The extent to which he relies on the "natural order of things" is shown by the fact that he is hardly aware of the threat posed by the highly advanced automatization of office procedures; he believes that everything will somehow fall into its accustomed place. The salaried employees are much more out of touch with reality than the workers: the available experience leaves no doubt that automation in offices will completely destroy their old, hierarchical structure.

The resignation and scepticism prevalent among the workers today are due to the feeling that everything they have won can be quickly lost, even before their dreams are realized. It is significant that the qualified skilled workers with above-average pay are the most dissatisfied ones. Hand in hand with this resignation and scepticism goes the perpetuation of traditional behaviour patterns which no longer correspond to the actually existing and legally guaranteed opportunities for the worker's social advancement. An example is the still deeply ingrained hostility to education which persists in working class families, who frequently refuse to avail themselves of professional or, in some cases, academic training for their children. But this attitude is not only a clear symptom of the resignation with which workers regard a "bourgeois-capitalist-liberal" society; it is also symptomatic of the standards of that society: by earning money quickly without a lengthy period of further education one hopes to acquire as soon as possible the outward signs of prosperity and thus acquire social prestige. Traditional behaviour patterns also militate against a ready acceptance of the idea that rational and purposeful planning for the future should take precedence over the impulsive and immediate gratification of a person's needs. Another element in this chain is the stubborn adherence to outmoded labour ethics, though other factors no doubt play a part in this attitude: opposition to sensible reductions of working hours frequently originates among the workers themselves.

Those who accept the conditions of modern production as unalterable tend to lay great stress on the therapeutic effects of leisure. But it is a dangerous illusion to hope that

additional leisure will automatically cure the damage caused
by work which is felt to lack purpose. The functional relations
between work and leisure are extremely important. As long as
one area of human existence—work—remains entirely determined by external forces, it will be difficult to achieve a state
of affairs in which the other area—leisure—can be made to
serve man's efforts to realize his full potential. Nor can the
problem be solved by making a man a shareholder in an
industrial concern, or by giving him a car or a house of his
own; these are no substitute for the rightful place which he
wishes to achieve in society.

At the same time we must not overlook the fact that
additional leisure and increased possibilities of consumption
can play a positive, almost revolutionary role in the democratization of our society : a person who learns to choose
between alternatives (watching TV or listening to records,
a holiday or a down-payment on a house) experiences a very
real freedom together with the consequences of such freedom,
i.e. the possibility of making the wrong choice; in a down-to-
earth and realistic way, he is learning to practise democracy.

Hitherto our society has failed to model itself on the pattern
of democratic partnership. On the contrary, the prevailing
pattern helps to perpetuate hierarchic, quasi-military habits
of thought and conduct, not only at our places of work but
in society and government generally; it perpetuates the
dichotomy of the few "up above" who go on doing what
they want, and the many "down below" who foot the bill; it
encourages some people to adopt a position of individualistic,
inward-looking self-sufficiency, and others to imitate blindly
what everyone else is supposed to be doing.

There is no doubt that in our society as at present constituted there exists an almost inconceivable discrepancy
between technological achievement, social progress and
human consciousness.

2. The SPD and the KPD after 1945

Immediately after the collapse of the national-socialist dictatorship in the spring of 1945, the Social Democrats all over
Germany set out to rebuild their party—the Social Demo-

cratic Party of Germany. They had no doubt whatsoever that, in view of the historico-political developments, the hour had struck when Socialism would come into its own. Breitscheid's prophetic words of 1932 : "After Hitler—we" would at last come true.

> The Social Democratic Party is the only party in Germany which has without compromise held fast to the great guiding lines of democracy and peace. This is why it alone can say that the principles of its policy have stood the test of history. All other movements in Germany are to blame, to a greater or lesser extent, for the rise of Nazism ... If the Social Democrats now claim the leadership in the building of a new German state, they do so not from self-seeking party motives. They have no intention to deprive, or attempt to deprive, other untainted and willing forces from their rightful share in this task. They only want an unambiguous answer to the question whether we, in Germany, wish to rebuild the old or build a new state. Among the bourgeois movements there are too many forces pressing for reconstruction rather than construction.

These words, imbued with deep socialist confidence, were written in summer 1945 by Kurt Schumacher who, in spite of having endured eleven years of great physical suffering in concentration camps, provided the decisive impetus which was to shape the party. Socialism for Schumacher was "the struggle for the spiritual, political and economic emancipation of the working man", "the struggle for justice and freedom against oppression and slavery"; he could not conceive of Socialism without democracy : "Democracy is inseparable from the concept and the ethics of Socialism"; Socialism and democracy together could alone provide the spiritual and political foundation for a "change of the economic and socio-psychological premisses of German politics" (quoted in Kaden, p. 72). Schumacher's unambiguous attitude served to check the re-emergence of the idea that "democracy matters little, Socialism is all", which had bedevilled the Socialists' relations to the Weimar Republic; the experience of totalitarianism made an affirmation of democracy imperative.

The indivisibility of Socialism and democracy enabled the SPD to come to a firm decision when the creation of a united workers' party was being discussed. Apart from the West German head-office of the SPD (camouflaged initially as "Dr. Schumacher's office") and the remainder of the executive-in-exile in London, there existed a so-called Berlin Central Committee (Grotewohl and Fechner) which also put in a claim to lead the party, though its influence did not extend beyond the Soviet-occupied zone. Not only in this Berlin Central Committee, but throughout the whole country, Social Democrats cherished the hope that the division of the German labour movement into two parties—the SPD and the KPD— would now wither away.

There are many explanations for this hope. Among them is the shock sustained in 1933, when the dynamics of the national-socialist "revolution" simply swept away the organizations of the labour movement which had for so long enjoyed the reputation of mythical indestructibility. Furthermore, under the immediate impact of the destruction of the state and the economy, certain attitudes, quite understandable in the context of 1945, became current among the population at large : among them was a deeply emotional sympathy for the proletarian revolutionaries in the East and an equally emotional aversion from the Western, capitalist victors who, in West Germany, tended to support forces which, anxious to restore the old capitalist order, were anti-socialist. Many people then felt that a re-orientation towards Russia gave hope of a new Europe, founded in the solidarity of nations hitherto neglected by history. The Soviet Union, risen from hunger, misery and agony to the position of a victorious power in a patriotic war of defence, was for many people, from the Right and Left alike, the example which they now sought. Compared to the Soviet Union, the West had little, if anything, to offer : freedom and democracy— concepts which were felt by the Germans of 1945 to be rather empty; they understood Stalin much better : "Hitlers come and Hitlers go, but the German nation goes on for ever".

This outlook was often rooted in nothing more solid than the fear of a confrontation with the past or an attempt to escape from the demands of reality into a pseudo-revolutionary dream. The fact remains that—notwithstanding the political decisions of the SPD leadership after 1945—these ideas prevented German Socialists from making a realistic assessment of the Soviet-communist ideology and practice. In spite of the persecution of the Social Democrats in the Soviet-occupied zone after the compulsory unification of the SPD and the KPD, there was still much wishful thinking: that it must be possible to transcend the present, admittedly horrifying reality, and arrive at "pure" Communism; that in spite of all differences it must be possible "to make everyone's sincere convictions into a basis for common political aspirations" (Kaden, p. 238). These attitudes are easy to understand when we remember the idealistic and humanitarian view of man and society traditionally held by the socialist labour movement.

Though he believed in the historical necessity of "a single labour party including all occupations and strata", Kurt Schumacher rejected a *rapprochement* with the Communists with his usual firmness and intransigence. He regarded the KPD "not as a German class party, but as a foreign state party", whose theory and practice were entirely dictated by the Soviet Union. Schumacher objected to a merger with the KPD not only on national, but even more strongly on fundamentally democratic grounds. Socialism without democracy, without humanity and freedom of thought was not Socialism as he understood it: "Just as the idea of the Germans being a chosen master race must vanish, so the idea of the dictatorship of the proletariat must also disappear", he wrote in the Berlin *"Tagesspiegel"* in April 1946, shortly before the compulsory unification of the KPD and the SPD in the Eastern zone. At this juncture the entire SPD in the Western zones shared his view that the unification of the two parties was nothing but "an extraordinarily brutal attempt by the Communist leaders to capture the Social Democratic Party". Thus even before the partition of Germany had entered into the political consciousness of the people, Schumacher took it upon himself to divide the SPD for the sake of democracy. The London party executive took the same attitude.

As early as 1945 Schumacher tried to mark out his party's future path in one other respect; he tried to determine the

extent to which democratically conceived Socialism should
have national connotations. In this question too he agreed
with his political friends in exile. At first sight it may appear
that Schumacher was prompted by mainly tactical considerations: in 1945 it might have seemed impossible to subdue
Germany's aggressive nationalism without consistently pursuing her national interests. But the issue had deeper roots:
they lay in Schumacher's basic convictions which were those
of a Prussian-German patriot. All the elements of his theoretical conceptions logically flow from these convictions and can
be explained by his emotional commitment to them. Like
Lassalle, Schumacher considered national self-determination
to be the precondition of freedom, democracy and Socialism
in Germany; he considered internationalism inconceivable
unless it rested upon national patriotism and a "basis of a
national world-order". Those who thought differently were,
according to him, not Germans, but "Russians", "Separatists"
or even "Chancellors of the Allies". Like Lassalle, he also
combined his Prusso-German patriotism with the idea of the
historical mission of the German labour movement; for the
first time in its history, its social interests and aims completely
coincided with those of the nation. More than that: in the
historic situation of 1945, the SPD alone was capable of
articulating the interests of the nation.

In Schumacher's conception of a nationally committed
Socialism, the German Social Democrats found the belated
fulfilment of their desire to identify themselves with the
nation, a desire which neither the old Empire nor the Weimar
Republic had ever fully satisfied. Yet at this very time the
idea of a national state was undergoing a tangible deprecia-
tion. The national orientation of the SPD's political ideas after
1945 made it much more difficult for the party to find its
way into Europe, to acquire an international outlook, and to
recognize the most pressing tasks which confront it in the
second half of the 20th century.

In relation to yet another problem, in which tradition
played an equally important part, the SPD succeeded in
changing its old outlook. The problem was the party's attitude
to the doctrines of Karl Marx. Marx's methodology, his conception of history, and his economic predictions were subjected

to scrutiny, particularly in theoretical journals such as *"Das sozialistische Jahrhundert"* (Berlin), *"Sozialistische Monatshefte"* (Stuttgart), *"Volk und Staat"* (Karlsruhe), and *"Sozialistische Tribüne"* (Frankfurt a.M.). Some socialist theoreticians continued to apply Marx's historical materialism and his philosophico-historical sociological methods without modification; others not only rejected the content of the marxist doctrine, but denied the relevance of the heuristic principle on which the doctrine rested. But nearly everyone agreed that while some essential parts of Marx's theory of economic development (e.g. the theory of the concentration of capital) were confirmed by events, others, explicable only from the perspective of a certain time and place, were of only historical interest. Marx's doctrines as a whole could no longer claim the rank and importance of an incontrovertible dogma; yet Marx's method of reasoning, as used by him for an understanding of the historical situation and for the application of analytical results to concrete tasks, was seen to retain its unimpaired validity. In contrast to Kautsky's deterministic interpretation of marxist doctrines, emphasis was now laid on the role played by the organized will of like-minded people in the historical development towards Socialism :

> In his book *"Jenseits des Kapitalismus"*, which was much discussed at the time, Paul Sering writes : "The motives of the socialist struggle were and remain the same before and after Marx : the will to free man from his subjection to personal oppression and from the impersonal forces of supply and demand, the desire for social justice, the belief in the possibility of a system built upon the fraternal co-operation of the workers rather than on the mindless co-existence of ants. Scientific analysis can reveal the conditions under which these goals can be realized, and the forces on which this realization depends. But these forces cannot prevail unaided; they need the actions and the will of men. No struggle has an inevitable outcome as far as necessity, such as is known to history, is concerned . . ." (p. 21).

Prior to 1933 Schumacher had modelled his views on those of Fichte and Lassalle. He did not acquire a positive attitude to Marx till after 1945. He does not regard Marx's doctrines as dogmata or edifices of theorems, but admits the validity of Marx's methods of political and economic analysis; he sees in Marxism neither the sole motive nor the only means towards an understanding of Socialism; instead, he acknowledges a pluralism of motivation leading to Socialism.

Schumacher's idea that the SPD must learn to think of itself as a people's party is closely connected with his recognition of a pluralism of motivations. While he continued to recognize that the class of industrial workers was the mainspring of the SPD's power, he felt that the party must shoulder the task of making the middle class democratic. Experience in the Weimar period had shown that democracy cannot be safeguarded unless the middle classes acquire a democratic outlook. Nor could Socialism be put into practice unless the middle strata (under which heading Schumacher included office workers, farmers, tradesmen and intellectuals) became converted. The technological changes in production methods and their effect upon the social and economic structure tended to accelerate the assimilation of the workers to the middle strata, or at least to blur the former demarcation lines between them; industrial workers could therefore no longer hope to win a majority at the polls (quite apart from the fact that the SPD, confined to the Western zones, had lost its richest catchment area in Central Germany).

It was not possible, in 1945, "to give the old party a new face" (quoted in Kaden, p. 284); instead of a new SPD, the old party was recreated: "With the full weight of its long history behind it, the party re-entered public life" (Kaden, p. 281). The leading role in the reconstruction of the party's organization and in the shaping of its political image fell in the main to those who, having held office in the party in the years before 1933, had remained in Germany; they had had little or no share in the critical reflexions of the leaders who had spent the war years abroad or in the penitentiaries and concentration camps of the National Socialists; in their ideas of Socialism and their view of the world they took up the threads where they had been left in 1933. The members and officials who formed the party's organizational backbone in 1945 had been completely cut off from international development for twelve years; the influence exerted by the emigrés and by the socialist parties abroad was also extremely small at the time. In rebuilding the SPD these members and officials had no other model but their memories of the Weimar period. The new members, who joined the party after 1945, acquired little political importance beyond their local sphere of influence; in many instances the best of the older officials moved into parliament, government posts or public administration.

The party life which thus gradually emerged was moulded upon the old pattern, a pattern set by the pride in the party's traditions, loyalty to the leaders, a mistrust of the state, the entrepreneur, the Church and the intellectuals, and a pseudo-revolutionary, emotion-inspired radicalism. All this left little room for a scrutiny of the outmoded ideological posture of the party, for new ways of thinking or for the spontaneous expression of a "socialist will to act" such as Schumacher demanded. The disappointment of many new members in the old party can be gauged from its development between 1947 and 1950: membership figures dropped from 875,479 to 683,896.

The full weight of the old traditional impediments soon made itself felt in the politics of the SPD. The radical phraseology was again pitted against a reluctance to act spontaneously outside parliament. An example is the SPD's struggle against re-armament: though denying the right of parliament to decide on Germany's contribution, the party refrained from boycotting the relevant debates in parliament and did not mobilize the power of the workers' organizations outside it. The chasm between dogmatic intransigence in matters of principle and a ready acceptance of political responsibility yawned once again. While in parliament Schumacher steered the unswerving course of intransigent opposition, the SPD played a considerable part in the political and social reconstruction on the Land and local levels, quite apart from its loyal efforts in parliament itself to give democratic shape to laws which it opposed on principle. Instead of deriving guidance for the future from the results of scientific political analysis, the SPD was content passively to await future developments. Indulging in wishful thinking, it nursed for a long time the idea that the capitalist reconstruction of Germany would necessarily end in a crisis which would automatically bring the SPD to power.

Between 1947 and 1960 the SPD's policies—its opposition in the Economic Council in 1947, its collaboration in the Parliamentary Council, and, from 1949 onwards, its renewed opposition in the Federal Parliament against the government's policies on Europe, German unity and particularly on rearmament—reflected two things : firstly a faulty grasp of political realities and secondly the party's inability to make its opposition intelligible and convincing to the German voter by pointing out its actual achievements and its inherent importance in the democratic process.

When a merger of the KPD and the SPD had been prevented in West Germany the KPD there did not at first put itself forward as a radical, revolutionary party, but as an anti-fascist, democratic party fighting "for the national unity of Germany and for a just peace". It claimed that its path to Socialism was of a special, German kind. By means of these tactics it achieved considerable successes in the first Land elections and filled several ministerial posts in the first postwar Land governments. The thesis about a special, German way to Socialism was abandoned in 1948 (when the same issue led to an open breach between Yugoslavia and the Soviet Union); henceforth the Soviet model was unconditionally accepted and the revolutionary class struggle once more given its prominent position in the party's policy. Concurrently with this political *Gleichschaltung,* the party carried out internal purges of actual or potential dissidents.

In 1949 the KPD rejected the Basic Law but participated in the first general elections for the Federal Parliament; the poor results (5·7 per cent, 15 seats) led to an attempt to combine the revolutionary class struggle with national resistance; the National Front, led by the KPD, was to oppose not only the "Allied colonial powers", but also their helpers, the German bourgeoisie. The goal of the KPD's tactics and politics—frequently stated in public after July 1952—was the abolition of the existing social and political order in the Federal Republic by extra-parliamentary means, by a "revolutionary overthrow of the Adenauer régime"; the chief means to be employed was the political mass strike. Not till April 1956, when the Federal Constitutional Court was already adjudicating on the alleged unconstitutionality of the KPD, did the party revoke its statements about the "revolutionary overthrow" of the existing parliamentary democracy. At this stage the KPD tried to exploit the parliamentary system; this was in itself unrealistic, since the party had no seats in the Federal Parliament and was only represented in two Land Diets (in Bremen and Lower Saxony with a total of six deputies). On 17 August 1956 the Federal Constitutional Court declared the Communist Party unconstitutional and dissolved forthwith; since then—apart from several front organizations— the KPD in the Federal Republic exists as an underground party; it seeks in particular to establish its cadres in large concerns. The ban on the party makes it more difficult than ever to enter into an open debate with these small, but politically very committed groups and with their sympathizers.

The SPD and the KPD achieved the following results in the general elections for the Federal Parliament between 1949 and 1965:

	1949	1953	1957	1961	1965	
	131	151	169	190	202	seats
SPD	6.935	7.945	9.446	11.427	12.813	million votes
	29.2	28.8	31.8	36.2	39.3	per cent of votes
	15	–				seats
KPD	1.362	0.608				million votes
	5.7	2.2				per cent of votes

Not till after its setbacks in the general elections of 1953 and 1957 did the SPD begin to gain a new insight into its own political problems. This new insight found expression in the Godesberg Programme of Principles of 1959. Kurt Schumacher's "intransigent opposition" had captivated the party to such an extent that ideological inadequacies and programmatic uncertainties could remain hidden. The Dortmund Programme of Action of 1952, with a preface written by Schumacher shortly before his death, clearly reflects this state of affairs: the SPD behaved as if it had an ideology, a political programme—as if it was successful. Even after his death Schumacher remained a kind of "ideology substitute";

only after it lost the election of 1953 did the party set itself in motion.

The old positions crystallized once again: the neo-marxist Left (e.g. the circle of *"Die Andere Zeitung"*, a paper founded in 1955 by Gleissberg, former editor of *"Vorwärts"*; among its contributors were Viktor Agartz and Wolfgang Abendroth) persisted in the opinion that the SPD's task, now as ever, was the transformation of the social system along socialist lines; they resisted all suggestions that the party should give up its traditions, pragmatically adapt itself to the existing system and turn into a party of reform as the Reformists demanded. The Left found support among those officials who opposed attempts at reform not so much on ideological grounds, but because of a certain mental inertia and a need for prestige; another reason was that the reformers were not only fighting against ideological prejudices but also attacking unsuccessful political practices and the ossification of the party machine.

Considerable differences existed between the various groups of reformers: there was the "radical" Right, distinguished by its impulsiveness, its contagious enthusiasm and light-hearted criticism, rather than by its ability to make a rational contribution to the analysis of the complex issues (e.g. the circle of Klaus-Peter Schulz in Berlin till about 1957). Taking up a more central position were those reformers who had no axe to grind either for or against tradition; they (e.g. W. Eichler, G. Weisser) wished to base the intellectual foundations of the party upon a scientifically established ethics on the lines propounded by Leonard Nelson; or they (e.g. C. Schmid, W. v. Knoeringen) wanted to see the political tasks of the party justified in the light of the trends of future development. *Erich Ollenhauer* (1901–1963) and Wilhelm Mellies, two of Schumacher's successors as party chairmen, tried to mediate between the different points of view; they were actuated not so much by political and ideological motives as by sentiment and a deep concern for the party organization. *Ernst Reuter* (1889–1953) and Willy Brandt took up a position which could be compared with that of the Reformists at the turn of the century: they emphasized political action, but stipulated

that it must rest on the basic socialist values which no interpretation can change. After the forfeited elections of 1953 and
shortly before his death, Reuter demanded a programme of
action which would "emphasize the positive goals of the
socialist movement". Such a programme was not even envisaged till after the elections of 1957; the SPD entered those
elections with a programme which seemed to conform to the
wishes of the electorate down to the last potential voter and
which did not offer a real alternative to the programme of
the ruling party; the SPD's slogan was "Security for All".
The loss of the 1957 elections led to more insistent demands
that the party should re-examine its own position in the light
of the structural changes in society. The resulting discussion
culminated in the Godesberg Programme which was adopted
in 1959.

This programme deliberately refrains from a specifically
socialist analysis of prevailing conditions; nor does it predict
a utopia founded on a philosophy of history. It was intended
to free the party from the traditional commitments which had
hampered its aspirations to become a popular party. While
acknowledging its obligations to Marx who had been the
German Social Democrats' mentor in philosophy, economics
and sociology, the party proposed to relegate his doctrines to
the status of historical documents. Thus the pluralism of
ethical motivation which is involved in the political option in
favour of democratic Socialism was now programmatically
formulated : "The Social Democratic Party ... is a community of men holding different beliefs and ideas. Their
agreement is based on the moral principles and political aims
they have in common".[1]

The aims of Socialism were no longer to be deduced from
unalterable ideological formulae; according to the Godesberg
Programme, democratic Socialism was to be understood as a
continuing task inherent in every historical situation and
always subject to reformulation; its unchangeable ethical
inspiration must be freedom, justice and solidarity—"the
basic values of socialist aspirations".

While Schumacher had still regarded the SPD as guardians
of "the interests of the working population" against the

[1] "Godesberg Programme", English edition, Bonn, 1960.

"autocratic, property-defending state", the Godesberg Programme changed this image so that it became increasingly the image of a popular party which seeks to integrate the manifold political interests of various social strata rather than having its social and political roots in one particular section of the community. The formulae: "Together—not against each other", and "Greater justice for all" express this outlook. The SPD also changed its political tactics, a change which was inaugurated by Herbert Wehner, one of the SPD's Vice-Chairmen, when he addressed Parliament in 1960: Schumacher's idea of an "intransigent" and total opposition on all political issues, an opposition which would constitute a genuine alternative to the ruling party, was replaced after Godesberg by emphasis on the common tasks of the government and the opposition, even though there could still be disagreement between them about the priorities assigned to various issues.

In terms of its voters and members, the SPD of today is no longer the workers' party which it was in the nineteenth century. Its leadership had always tended to include a high proportion of artisans and craftsmen, and was always slanted towards the petit-bourgeois and the academic. Today the industrial workers' share in the shaping of the party's image is much smaller than that of the members of the so-called "new middle class": office workers, civil servants, academics, self-employed persons, and above all, members of the so-called managerial class, including the municipal and welfare bureaucracy. But a numerical break-down of membership according to occupations shows a different picture. Members who joined the SPD between 1956 and 1961 fall into the following occupational and social categories: manual workers 55 per cent, salaried employees, 13.2 per cent, civil servants 7.6 per cent, self-employed 3.6 per cent, free-lance and academic professions 3.2 per cent, housewives 10.2 per cent, old age pensioners 6.1 per cent. (Quoted in Lohmar, p. 35, from information received from the SPD executive who consider that the same distribution among occupations applies to the party as a whole.)

Distribution of occupations among the followers of the SPD compared with the distribution among the population as a whole is shown in the following table:

	Manual workers	Non-manual workers	Civil servants	Self employed	Farmers and agric. workers	Independent means
Total population	39%	10%	8%	11%	14%	18%
SPD followers	60%	11%	6%	6%	2%	15%

(quoted from Viggo Graf Blücher: *"Der Prozess der Meinungsbildung—dargestellt am Beispiel der Bundeswahl, 1961"*, Emnid Survey, Bielefeld, 1962.)

The membership figures of the SPD from 1945 (end of year figures)

1946	711,448	1954	585,479	1962	646,584
1947	875,479	1955	589,051	1963	648,415
1948	846,518	1956	612,219	1964	678,484
1949	732,218	1957	626,189	1965	710,448
1950	683,896	1958	623,813	1966	733,004
1951	649,529	1959	534,254	1967	727,890
1952	627,817	1960	649,578		
1953	607,456	1961	644,780		

The path of the SPD after it had adopted the Godesberg Programme evoked both widespread approval and violent opposition. Some feel that the SPD had no alternative; others are of the opinion that it must go even further: since the classical swing of the pendulum seems to have been rendered inoperative by the consolidation of the government's position, and by the voters' reluctance to reward the opposition, the SPD must strive for a Great Coalition. The critics of the SPD, on the other hand, maintain that what had once been a democratic association whose members shared a common *Weltanschauung* has become a quasi-state institution run on hierarchic lines. According to these critics the party has become a kind of service organization which seeks to satisfy the needs of different consumers, and at the same time an organ of power. Others again regard the SPD as a party of reform within the framework of the established order, as an opposition which is of a piece with the system and corresponds to the authoritarian democracy of the Federal Republic. Yet others fear that the SPD, by conforming to the status quo and renouncing all attempts to change the structure of society, might put both democracy and party government into jeopardy; in their view a Great Coalition is a rudimentary form of a one-party state.

It is still too early to assess the full import of the SPD's development after 1960. A particularly difficult problem arises from the disintegration of the Left, which set in with the exclusion of marxist ideas from the Godesberg Programme, and came to a temporary halt at the end of 1961 with the rigorous truncation of the by no means consistently neo-marxist Left wing (SDS — German Socialist Students' League and their supporters). So far only tentative attempts have been made to create a new Left-wing party with a strictly non-communist ideology and organization. Nor have the trade unions been altogether successful in achieving a genuine and democratic integration of the radical Left-wing forces. Yet both industrial labour and the intelligentsia remain by no means unsusceptible to Left-wing attitudes. One wonders whether, in the interest of a stable democracy in Germany, the SPD can afford to overlook the fact that views and interests to the Left of the party are no longer represented by its ideology and policy.

The relations between the SPD and the trade unions have also undergone a change which almost amounts to a reversal of their respective roles. The SPD is increasingly reluctant to rely on the support of the trade unions for its policies, so as to avoid the slightest appearance of promoting sectional interests. The SPD and the trade unions are more and more growing apart, a trend which antedates the emergency legislation; their differences on questions of economic policy, as on the important question of an extension of co-determination, are of long standing.

The extent to which the SPD and the trade union movement are mutually dependent has always been greatly exaggerated by their opponents, particularly in the question of the unions' contributions to party funds. The unions have provided mainly organizational help for the SPD's candidates and deputies, and only occasionally contributed to election expenses of the constituency parties. The SPD, unlike the Christian Democratic Union/Christian Social Union (*Christlich-Demokratische Union/Christlich-Soziale Union* — CDU/CSU), largely raises its own finances from (graduated) membership fees, contributions from elected holders of public offices and from the income from its own publishing houses, presses and book shops which constitute a major stock company; this concern does not so much make direct contributions in cash, as allow considerable discounts.

Another difficult unresolved issue is the development of democracy within the SPD itself: while formally assured, this democracy appears to lack real content—a state of affairs which admittedly prevails to an even greater extent in the other parties.

This raises the question whether the members of any party today are in a position to participate in the formulation of policies. The choice of subjects for discussion, the manner in which meetings are organized, and the excessive emphasis on technical and organizational matters show that in the SPD too there is a tendency to reduce the political content of members' activities (only a small per cent of local parties submit resolutions to the party's congresses); the number of exclusive social gatherings grows; only 25 per cent of members attend meetings. The honorary party officials have virtually no influence (though their active help is of paramount importance to the party's survival); they find it increasingly difficult to explain the decisions made at the top to the voters, since they lack insight into the overall situation; the role of the party's bureaucracy, which remains both socially and professionally underprivileged, also seems to be diminishing.

The important special sub-committees of the SPD work in private and have no effect on public opinion. The congress has virtually no authority to take decisions; the executive have ceased to be the executive arm of the congress, and often take political decisions in advance which the legislative organs of the party can merely ratify; working groups (whose findings are not usually binding) and festive gatherings have replaced rigorous political debate at party congresses; altogether the party prefers to present a harmonious front to the public. These tendencies towards the erosion of inner party democracy not only reflect the autocratic aspirations of the top echelons; they also point to the failure of the members whose passivity often forces the leaders to take autocratic decisions.

If it is true that a major party simply can no longer afford exclusively to represent sectional interests, then the threat to inner party democracy may well grow to imperil democracy in general. For the function of politically integrating different social interests must extend to the alignments inside the party itself; it is there, in the pre-parliamentary stage, that political decisions are prepared; decisions reached on this level result in the party's general line which must reflect the compromise between various group interests within the party.

The tendency of the SPD to bring its own political ideas and aims largely into harmony with those of the CDU/CSU is already showing dubious results. Certain issues which should be brought into the open and discussed are at present taboo; among them are the question of the Eastern territories, the recognition of the Oder-Neisse line, and a realistic appraisal of the chances of Germany's re-unification.

The SPD's inclination to minimize tensions and conflicts has also prevented it from living up to Schumacher's claim that since 1945 democratic Socialism is *the* progressive political force in Germany. The party has not been able to root out value concepts which have always had a well-nigh traumatic effect on the German people; thus, e.g. the concept "nation"—abused and perverted by William II and Hitler—has never been sufficiently analyzed and clarified. By abstaining from a relentless analysis of the political, economic and cultural realities of the Federal Republic, the party has also failed to help work out long-term political guiding lines applicable to the complex world of today. All this may well disappoint and repel the younger generation, particularly the young intellectuals, and thus forfeit some of the SPD's genuine potential.

By its present strategy which tries to avoid, or to reconcile, social and political conflicts in state and society rather than bring them to a head, and by endeavours to achieve the maximum of homogeneity within the party itself, the SPD unintentionally aids and abets the authoritarian tendencies in Germany. Democracy must acknowledge the real and necessary existence of conflicting interests; the idea of a society without conflicts, and of the state as an authority placed above social groups whose conflicts it settles rests on an outlook

which smacks of authoritarianism and indeed of totalitarianism.

It is generally recognized that the SPD—like the CDU—
no longer possesses a consistent political philosophy. Though
both parties still adhere to ideological formulae, these are so
general and permissive that they can be adapted to suit day-
to-day purposes. This degeneration of ideology into formulae
is due to changes in the structure of society, to the fact that
class differences have become less pronounced and class-
consciousness has been reduced to some few typical attitudes.

Yet it would be wrong to underestimate the importance of
the remaining ideological "formulae" or "tatters". They have
become less a matter of reason than of emotion. They still
allow the citizen to appeal to virtually indubitable "truths";
he can then surround himself with ramparts made up of certain perennial attitudes and escape the task of reflecting
rationally upon political realities and of participating in the
dynamics of the political process.

We cannot escape this dilemma by clamouring for a
genuine, hard and fast, comprehensive ideology; such
clamour frequently hides a social infantilism, fear of an
apparently chaotic world, feelings of inferiority, irresoluteness
and immaturity—attitudes which have no proper place in a
democracy and which could easily assume totalitarian
features.

The formulation of a new, rigid and impervious doctrine,
comparable to the faith which inspired the labour movement
of the 19th century, is no real alternative to the SPD's present
purposeful pragmatism which quite legitimately aims at the
eventual capture of power. Yet the party should, at this time,
also remember its long-term aims which, though obscured by
the tactical demands of today, will set the pattern for the
future; it should have the courage to design a "realizable
utopia" adapted to the conditions of a modern industrial
society and rooted in socialist aspirations.

3. The German Trade Unions after 1945

In the second half of 1945 the German trade unions started
to rebuild their organizations, initially within individual con-

cerns and on a local level; at first, different regulations enforced by different occupying powers made it difficult to proceed to a more comprehensive regional organization. In November 1947 the trade unions in the British and American zones created a joint Trade Union Council which the trade unions in the French zone were later allowed to join. After November 1946 frequent meetings took place between trade-union leaders from the four occupied zones; attempts to combine with the Free German Trade Union Federation in the Soviet zone and to form a single all-German trade union federation failed.

This led, in October 1949, to the creation in Munich of the German Trade Union Confederation (*Deutscher Gewerkschaftsbund*—DGB) covering the area of the German Federal Republic; it included the sixteen industrial unions which had by then been established. These retained their organizational identity and their independent wages policies, but surrendered to the Confederation certain tasks and responsibilities as well as part of their income. The first chairman of the DGB, *Hans Böckler* (1875–1951), had sought to establish general unions for all occupations instead of industrial unions; his efforts were frustrated by the intervention of the occupying powers, particularly the British, who feared that powerful leaders of general unions might introduce an undemocratic element into German politics. Böckler was also unable to overcome the opposition of the officials of the miners' and steel workers' unions which had by then acquired considerable financial and industrial power in the Ruhr and on the Rhine.

An industrial trade union (*Industriegewerkschaft*—IG) which had formerly included all the skilled and unskilled workers of an industry, now also embraces all that industry's salaried staff. In 1964 the DGB had approximately 6·43 million members. Figures for the 16 existing industrial unions were as follows :

Metal	1,896,000
Public services, transport and communications	984,000
Chemicals, paper and pottery	523,000
Mining and power	480,000
Building, stone and soil	477,000
Railways	434,000

Textiles and clothing	337,000
Postal services	316,000
Food, entertainment, hotels	281,000
Printing and paper	146,000
Wood and timber	145,000
Commerce, banks, insurance	127,000
Education and science	91,000
Leather	84,000
Horticulture, agriculture and forestry	78,000
Arts	32,000

All the industrial unions as well as the DGB are strictly democratic in their structure; direct democracy is only exercised in cases of strikes, when every member votes.

After 1945 the former sharp ideological divisions in the trade union movement were at first avoided; it was intended that all working people would join together in a united movement "democratic in character and independent of employers, government, denomination or party". But the DGB did not remain the only organization of its kind for long. As early as 1949 a separate organization for salaried employees (*Deutsche Angestelltengewerkschaft*—DAG) sprang up whose aims are very similar to those of the DGB. The *Deutsche Beamtenbund,* embodying certain moderate features of corporate tradition, represents permanent civil servants. The *Christliche Gewerkschaftsbewegung* (CGB) was established in 1955; it has a distinctly ideological, i.e. christian, foundation.

In 1964 the DAG had 480,000 members (of whom 33·3 per cent were women, compared with the DGB's 16 per cent; the DGB comprises some 700,000 salaried employees (DGB total distribution : 79 per cent manual workers, 12 per cent salaried employees, 8 per cent civil servants). In 1964 676,000 civil servants belonged to the *Beamtenbund*.

After 1945 the German trade unions exercised a powerful attraction; when the DGB was founded in 1949 it already had 4·9 million members. The unions, regarded by the occupying powers as a crucial factor in the democratization of Germany, were felt to be the moving force behind the reconstruction of industry, production and the economy generally. In the minds of the workers they also assumed a political role; in particular, they offered to the many who for a variety of reasons had become disgusted with party politics an opportunity to be politically active, to collaborate in the restoration of the economic and political order. After 1945 a strong united trade-union movement appeared to many people to offer a guarantee for a stabilization of political and economic conditions in Germany under new, positive, democratic auspices.

Accordingly members responded readily not only to the union leaders' efforts for a united trade-union movement, but also to their desire to assume regulative political functions in order to give the state and society a new, anti-capitalist, socialist and democratic character.

The DGB's Principles of Economic Policy, formulated at its inaugural congress in 1949, clearly show the unions' self-confidence :

> The unions, being the organizations of manual workers, salaried employees and civil servants work for the economic, social and cultural interests of the working population. They support an economic system which will do away with social injustice and material poverty, and offer work and a livelihood to everyone willing to work ... Starting from this premiss, the unions make the following basic demands :
>
> I. An economic policy which, while preserving the dignity of all free men, will secure full employment for all those willing to work; the most efficient use of all national productive resources, and the satisfaction of the most important national economic needs.
>
> II. Co-determination by organized labour in all economic, social and personnel aspects of management.
>
> III. Nationalization of key industries, particularly mining, iron and steel, chemicals, power, essential transport and banking.
>
> IV. A fair share for all in the total national economic product, and adequate provisions for those unable to work because of age, disablement or sickness ...

The virtually revolutionary socialist spirit of the unions soon collapsed in the face of a reality in whose shaping they had little say. The task of reconstruction after 1945 was of such magnitude and demanded so many day-to-day political decisions, that there was hardly time to pause to consider fundamental structural social changes. Thus the unions

were not directly represented in the Economic Council constituted in June 1947; and in spite of the fact that after 1945
the works councils had far more influence on the actual
running of concerns than the entrepreneurs whose attitude
was one of enforced caution, the trade unions made no
attempt to use the councils to consolidate their own organization in individual plants; they also failed to organize the
works councils on a municipal or regional basis, which would
have given them the opportunity—missed in 1918–19—of
influencing the economic and political developments of the
country as a whole. The unions' fight for the Co-determination
and Industrial Organization Bill was not particularly successful; the threat of strikes alone prevented an erosion of rights
which they had acquired earlier. This clearly showed that a
new situation had arisen in which the employers had regained
both their dominant economic and political position and their
influence in the affairs of the state which, though committed
to a liberal, democratic outlook, remained neutral on social
issues. Thus the events of 1950–52 did not only concern the
narrower issues of co-determination, but raised the more
general question of the unions' social and political relevance
to the new democratic state.

The lost battle for genuine co-determination in a democratic
economy accelerated the process by which the unions became
more resigned and less politically involved in a structural
transformation of the society in the Federal Republic. The
old dichotomy between the unions' aim to transform society
and the need to adapt to existing conditions which were not
of their own making, a rift which had remained hidden under
the quasi-revolutionary enthusiasm of the year "zero",
emerged once more. At the same time the unions were gradually losing the sympathy and the encouragement which the
population had accorded them. As the individual's share in
the "German economic miracle" grew, so the anti-capitalist
attitudes, which in 1945 had almost been a matter of course,
turned into an uncritical approval of the republic's neo-
capitalist economic system. By the same token there was a
growing uneasiness about the unions which were known to
be organizing the workers in a manner which made them
into dreaded social rivals and a political power in the land.

Nevertheless, between 1953 and 1955, it seemed once more as if the unions were poised for an ideological advance. In a speech, delivered at the Frankfurt congress of 1954 by Dr. Viktor Agartz, director of the trade unions' Institute for Economic Research—(*Wirtschaftswissenschaftliches Institut*-WWI), he formulated the idea of a trade union radicalism whose core was a theory of an "expanding wages policy".

> We need an expanding wages policy not only to raise the living standards of the working population, but to protect ourselves against inflation and to secure full employment... It is not enough to raise real wages so that they catch up with economic development. A wages policy must stimulate economic growth, so that a planned increase in consumer demand provokes an expansion of production. (*"Mitteilungen des WWI"*, 1953, No. 12.)
>
> Agartz also demanded a reorganization of some basic industries by turning them into autonomous corporations, increased co-determination in high-level industrial consultations by a re-organization of the Chambers of Commerce, and the creation of a Federal Economic Council. He rejected both part-ownership and profit sharing.

Agartz's proposals, which seemed to promise the implementation of the ideas of 1949, met with a ready response among union officials (not so much at the top as in the middle and at the grass roots); this at first disguised the fact that his success was no more than a fictitious victory. His idea—the idea of a comprehensive Union Socialism—allocated to the unions the political role of a radical socialist party; but it failed to provide a factual analysis of existing society and a realistic assessment of the unions' position within state and society. In certain crucial respects it also neglected the unions' own view of their role: they felt that being responsible for the workers' interests in society, they had to function as an integral part of that society and carry on under existing conditions while trying to increase the scope of democratic action.

This view probably inspired the ideas advanced by *Otto Brenner* (b. 1907), the Chairman of *IG Metall* and "uncrowned king" of a large section of the German trade unions. From 1956 onwards, Brenner tried to carry out a meaningful union policy which would avoid the extremes of unlimited accommodation on the one hand and of impotent resignation on the other while at all times raising the workers' demands to the very limits of what was feasible; he endeavoured to maximise the unions' effectiveness within the already set social and political pattern. While Brenner's trade-union "maximalism" can hardly be said to have inaugurated an ideological renaissance, it represents a rudimentary attempt at a trade-union theory of political action. We must also remember that their repeated failures to reform society made the leaders of the major industrial unions reluctant to abandon the secure and promising pastures of higher wages and shorter hours. (In this respect Brenner was no exception.)

These were the conditions which allowed *Ludwig Rosenberg* (b. 1903) to win the unions' approval for a revision of their programme, a revision which he had envisaged since 1959 and which Otto Brenner accepted with silent resignation; basically it meant falling into line with the programmatic re-orientation which the SPD had carried out in 1959. In November 1963 at Dusseldorf, a new Programme of Principles was launched, supplemented in March 1965 by a Programme of Action.

Rosenberg, Chairman of the DGB since 1962, is also a stern critic of the "sham idea of the market economy" which may bring prosperity to all but fails to secure justice for all. This view underlies his formulation of the economic and social purposes of the trade unions; but he always accepts as given the capitalist structure of the economy and the parliamentary democracy; he acknowledges the responsibility of the unions within the existing system, and consciously rejects the methods of political radicalism.

Georg Leber, Chairman of IG Building, Stone and Soil, goes even further than Rosenberg; he carries the idea of conformity to the capitalist system to such an extreme that the unions become for him "components of the system" constitutionally "endowed with public duties" and with certain important, quasi-corporate functions.

The Basic Law does not explicitly mention trade unions; they are referred to only in Article 9(3) which provides freedom of association and stipulates that employed persons are free to combine only through trade unions. But this privileged position of the unions is restricted by the absence of any mention of their right to a political strike; furthermore, compulsory membership in unions is stated to be unconstitutional. Since the unions' legal position is only negatively defined, every action which goes beyond this prescribed position necessarily brings them up against the bounds of the Constitution. This was soon confirmed when the unions tried to use their right to strike in the fight for co-determination.

The right of employees to have a voice in determining their working conditions is without any doubt a democratic right, and a strike is a means of realising this right. Political strikes are certainly a legitimate form of demonstration, for instance when matters of vital importance to the unions are being debated in parliament; but a militant political strike (a general strike) can, in the unions' own view, only be used to uphold or to win democracy.

The DGB describes itself in its statute as democratic and "independent...of parties" and has never abandoned this position in principle. The unions' political aims tend traditionally to correspond more closely to those of the SPD than to those of the CDU/CSU. Nevertheless, tensions have arisen between the unions and the SPD, e.g. in their approach to the question of co-determination, and, more recently, to the emergency legislation. The unions' personal links with the SPD are very much closer than with the CDU/CSU.

The trade unions' parliamentary representation since 1949 is given in the following table (cf. Kurt Hirche, *"Gewerkschafter im 5. Deutschen Bundestag"*, *Gewerkschaftliche Monatshefte*, 12, 1965):

	1949	1953	1957	1961	1965
Number of deputies, including Berlin	420	506	519	521	518
(i) those belonging to unions	115	194	202	223	242
those in (i) belonging to CDU/CSU	22	47	46	41	51
those in (i) belonging to SPD	80	142	154	179	188
Remaining parties, from 1961 only FDP	13	5	2	3	3

	1949	1953	1957	1961	1965
those in (i) belonging to DGB unions	106	168	172	185	197
those in (i) belonging to other unions	9	26	30	38	45

In 1953 the DGB ran into a crisis which arose from complaints that the christian unions were both numerically and politically underrepresented in it—though this was mainly due to their own (particularly the Protestants') political inertia; at the time the political activities of the DGB also openly conflicted with the policies of the CDU (re-armament). The attack was led by the Catholic Workers' Movement supported by a conservative minority of the Protestant Workers' Movement; leading christian trade unionists, e.g. Jakob Kaiser and Karl Arnold, soon dissociated themselves from this attack; the reaction of the Church leaders was also very cautious. The rebellious minority of christian trade-union leaders (following another electoral victory of their party) demanded parity on the DGB's representative bodies (which would have destroyed democracy within the unions), and an amendment of the 1949 Munich Programme of Principles to make it correspond more closely to their reformist ideas. The crisis, whose background was political rather than ideological, was weathered; nevertheless, in October 1953, the Christian-Social Fellowship was formed within the DGB. Two years later, in October 1955, the German Christian Trade Union Movement was launched; the initiative came from the International Confederation of Christian Trade Unions; neither the christian wing of the DGB, led by Kaiser and Arnold, nor the Catholic and Protestant Church leaders approved of this separation.

While the tensions inside the trade unions have lost the acuteness which characterized them during the 'fifties, they can hardly be said to have diminished : they no longer only concern the inadequate representation of the christian elements in the DGB, but relate to a wider question : must the unions abstain from politics in the wider sense if they are to avoid the danger of party bias?

The work of the trade unions was at one time hampered by internal communist opposition in the DGB; the unions' activities in the workshop often proved too weak to withstand communist pressures. The banning of the KPD in 1956 evoked no reaction among the unions' leadership. For the unions it meant the elimination of a radical faction which received its instructions from outside. But the ban certainly did not solve the increasingly urgent problem of how to integrate the communist workers; it still bedevils trade union activity at shop-floor level. It is in the interest of democracy that the trade unions should absorb the communist workers both politically and socially; as yet no party or organization has shown itself equal to this task.

The party-political independence of the trade unions is often wrongly held to imply the need for complete political abstention. The unions have in fact opposed the policies of the government and of the parties represented in the government on fundamental issues such as re-armament, the German army's use of atomic weapons, and emergency powers legislation. But in no instance have they attacked the constitutional order, much less advocated opposition against the state; they have in fact become politically effective within the framework of a free and democratic system. Unless the unions are politically articulate, they cannot afford the workers the necessary social protection, let alone fulfil the more general function of shaping the social system.

The old definitions of unions—as a class movement or a professional body, as a regulator in the labour market or a militant revolutionary force—are today largely superseded. This can be seen in the criticism which is levelled against the unions. They are blamed for becoming tame and integrated, a part of the new capitalism to which they not only conform but lend their support; by assuming responsibilities in the existing system they are said to lose sight of their real purpose which is to transform society. Others say that the unions have become so powerful and well organized that they advance their sectional interests regardless of the common weal, and have become a danger to a free, democratic society.

Modern industrial society no longer finds its political expression exclusively in parliamentary politics but also through other organized groups. Those who see an irreconcilable conflict between the state and organized sectional interests conceive democracy in terms of the classical liberal theory or of state authoritarianism. In order to guard both the state and the organized groups themselves against their power becoming absolute we need a multiplicity of organized interests enjoying equal rights; co-operating or competing, they represent the different social forces in a community *vis à vis* the state and guarantee a free and democratic settlement of social and political conflicts.

These reflections help us to define those of the trade unions' functions which relate to the shaping of society: first and foremost, the unions must strive for the greatest possible integration of the wage and salary earners as a condition of extending the scope of democratic action in the community. While they must recognize their share of responsibility for the existing system, they must not allow themselves to be absorbed into it without conflict. They must continue to discharge their concrete, everyday tasks, but must at the same time seek to reform and transform the social and economic system. By virtue of their democratic, humanitarian traditions and of their self-awareness they are better fitted for the task of changing society than any other organized group. But they too still have to overcome a great many inhibiting factors rooted in their lagging awareness and their incorrect assessment of political realities.

In the first place they must overcome the stagnation which besets their recruitment of new members. In 1958 the DGB had only 7·1 per cent more members than in 1951, while the number of persons employed rose during the same period by 22·8 per cent. The unions have obviously failed to penetrate into groups which had by tradition been largely closed to them (salaried employees, civil servants, women); nor have they gained a secure foothold in the tertiary sector (transport, services, commerce, banking, insurance) which is notoriously difficult to organize and included approximately 38 per cent of all persons employed in 1964; the fluctuations of membership are noteworthy: they were undoubtedly due to the unions' paying insufficient attention to the passive members. The unions still lack a coherent idea on which to base their shop-floor activities, a programme centring around the individual plant or concern which is such a vital factor in the life of the working man and could be used as a lever to overcome the imperfect democratization of society as a whole. In this context we must also mention the negative effects of co-determination which in its present form does not serve the implementation of the trade unions' economic policy. The workers' representatives have identified themselves to a surprising extent with the fate of their factory or concern: nowhere does the employer find greater understanding for his problems than among the works councils concerned with co-determination; there is far too little readiness to take on real responsibility and too little militancy on behalf of the workers' interests; the employees lack adequate training for the tasks which they should discharge in this context.

The problem of democracy in the unions themselves is particularly difficult. Though the federal structure of the IGs and of the DGB acts to prevent a one-sided concentration of power, the position of the DGB, and particularly of its top leadership, seems too weak by comparison with that of the IGs; this militates against a co-ordination of the trade unions' more far reaching policies. An even more serious problem is the trade unions' obvious tendency to become too bureaucratic; this leads to a growing divergence of interests between the leaders and the led, and means that members find it increasingly difficult to make their voice heard at the top; this in turn leads to widespread apathy. Broader democratic participation in opinion formation and decision making could reverse this trend. This is of vital importance not only to the trade unions but to democracy generally.

4. The SED and the Trade Unions in the Other Germany

In May 1945 some Social Democrats in Berlin tried to persuade leading members of the KPD to form a united socialist workers' party; they met with a refusal. It later became obvious that this refusal did not mean that the KPD leaders wanted to introduce the Soviet system in the Russian occupied zone at once; they intended first to seek allies among the various anti-fascist circles in Germany, to allay the suspicions of the Western allies and thereby make it possible to exert political influence in the other occupied zones. In its first proclamation, issued on 11 June 1945, the KPD represented itself as an anti-fascist, national, democratic party.

By the end of 1945 the KPD leaders had already changed their tactics; under the guise of democrats, they had by then occupied all the key positions in the government and the economy of the Soviet-occupied zone. The results of the first post-war elections in Austria and Hungary had disappointed the Communists' expectations, while the Social Democrats had scored notable successes. A similar outcome was feared in Germany : the after-effects of the National Socialists' anti-bolshevik propaganda, seemingly confirmed by the conduct of the Soviet occupation troops, together with the confidence which even traditionally non-socialist sections of the population reposed in the SPD whose demands at the time were more radical than those of the KPD, led the Communist leaders to press—from November 1945 onwards—for an amalgamation of the KPD and the SPD. At Easter 1946 the two parties in the Soviet-occupied zone finally merged into the Socialist Unity Party of Germany (*Sozialistische Einheitspartei Deutschlands*—SED). Members of both parties in many localities had spontaneously supported the KPD's case for a merger; they had not overcome the trauma caused by the split between the two parties before 1933; where the proposal met with scepticism or opposition, pressure and even terror were used by the occupying Soviet authorities.

Till 1949 the leaders of the SED upheld the fiction that in the new party the SPD and the KPD had met half-way; but after that date the SED set out to become a "leninist-type" party. In accordance with Lenin's conception, the SED constitutes an élite which stands above class and nation; by representing itself as such the party reveals its totalitarian character; this is also reflected in the party's organization which is based on the principle of so-called "democratic centralism"; it means that a minority of leaders at the centre rules over the majority along lines which, by Lenin's own admission, are those of military discipline.

The structure of the party's top leadership is also based on the principle of centralism. The congress, which meets every four years, formally elects the central committee; the central committee (in this as in all other instances briefed beforehand) "elects" the Politbureau to direct the political work between plenary sessions, and a Secretariat to deal with day-to-day work. Real power rests with these two bodies and not with the politically insignificant central committee. They dominate the entire government machine; the Secretariat is divided into sections which correspond to the departmental structure of the government and are the real power behind the various ministries. The central committee issues directives disguised as recommendations to the cabinet and the Chamber of Deputies. There is a considerable overlap between personalities and functions (e.g. Ulbricht, who is first secretary of the central committee, also presides over the cabinet, and thus rules both the party and the state). The party's dictatorship pervades the government and the administration on all levels.

The ruling party brooks no opposition and will not tolerate factions. Dissident groups and individuals are purged; thus in 1951 the SED expelled 150,000 of its members, mostly Social Democrats and old KPD members who opposed the transformation of the SED into a leninist-type party. The leadership of the party is similarly subject to periodic purges; thus in 1950 Paul Merker was expelled from the central committee, followed in 1952 by Franz Dahlem, second in command to Ulbricht (rehabilitated in 1956). After 17 June 1953 Wilhelm Zaisser (Minister for State Security) and Rudolf Herrnstadt (editor-in-chief of *"Neues Deutschland"*) were first ousted from the central committee and then expelled from the party. In 1958 Karl Schirdewan (member of the central committee and close collaborator of Ulbricht), Fred Oelssner (one of the party's theoreticians) and Ernst Wollweber (former Minister of State Security) were disciplined. All of them had opposed Ulbricht's uncompromising policies and advocated reforms and a certain amount of liberalization.

The opposition of the party's intelligentsia hinged on more fundamental issues. An example is the group which centred around the philosopher Ernst Bloch (he left East Germany in 1961), who advocated a "humane Socialism" as opposed to the Stalinist dogmatism of Ulbricht; the group included the physicist Robert Havermann (censured by the party in 1964) and the economic historian Jürgen Kuczynski. Wolfgang Harich (sentenced to ten years hard labour in 1957, released in 1965) and his friends exemplified the revisionist tendencies in the SED; they described their views which, though communist, were hostile to the SED, as follows :

> We do not wish to break with Marxism-Leninism; but we want to free it of Stalinism and dogmatism, and bring it back to its humanist and undogmatic ideas ... We want to reform the party from the inside ... The theory of Marxism-Leninism must be supplemented and enlarged by the insights of Trotsky, Bukharin ... Rosa Luxemburg and, to some extent ... Karl Kautsky. We must also incorporate that which is of value in the ideas of Fritz Sternberg and other social-democratic thinkers. We must use the knowledge and experience gained by Yugoslavia ... and the new ideas which have emerged from the theoretical discussions in Poland and China ..."
> (quoted in Weber, *"Der Deutsche Kommunismus"*, pp. 599, 601).

As early as the middle of 1945 Ulbricht himself began to rebuild the trade unions in the Soviet zone; but not even at this early stage were they given the right to co-determination in the factory or at higher levels or allowed to influence wages policies and working conditions. The works councils, acting as the mouthpiece of the employees, frequently opposed the SED's efforts to introduce politics into industry; they were abolished in 1948 and replaced by trade-union councils in the workshops (*Betriebsgewerkschaftsleitung*—BGL). In 1950 the Communist Trade Union Confederation (FDGB) expressly acknowledged the leading position of the SED in its statute. According to this statute, the SED constitutes the "leading force of all organizations of the working class and of the working people generally, and of state and social organizations"; this entitles it to use mass organizations to transmit its will to the masses. The primacy which it claims for itself is translated into practice either by the exercise of direct influence or by special party groups within the mass organizations; the party's statute imposes on members the duty to carry out the party's directives and decisions within the other organizations to which they belong. The structure of the trade unions corresponds to that of the party on all levels : the chairman of the executive of the FDGB usually belongs to the corresponding echelon of the party, so that the party's leading role is always assured.

Membership of the FDGB is not officially compulsory; but to opt out amounts to an act of defiance against the régime, and entails the loss of many important social benefits; as a result, 6.3 million of a total of 6.5 million working people belonged to trade unions in 1962.

Unlike the SED, the FDGB has no direct influence on the government machine and disposes of no direct means of sanctions in the state. It cannot therefore be called a "state trade union" in the strict sense, and must rely mainly on ideological persuasion and a differentiated system of social pressures, privileges and inducement. Trade-union activity centres on so-called production tasks assigned to individual enterprises. The Labour Code of 1961 (§ 12) enumerates the functions of the unions:

1. Promotion of socialist competition.
2. Application of more modern methods.
3. Collaboration in collective bargaining.
4. Application of the socialist principles of achievement.
5. Participation in the affairs of the cadres.
6. Development of cultural and sports activities.
7. Accident prevention and the protection of health.
8. Elimination of shortcomings in individual enterprises.

The trade-union organization in individual plants is thus regarded as the "basis of the trade unions"; it includes all the trade-union members of the plant and is headed by the BGL. All management functions and overall responsibility are vested in the director, who "manages the enterprise according to the principle of exclusive leadership. He is held personally responsible for the fulfilment of the tasks assigned to the plant" (Labour Code). The trade unions thus do not even have an influence on the economic aspects of the production plan, though they are responsible for the political and ideological promotion of it (the director is only partly responsible for "political and ideological education"). The unions and the management work for the same master—the "state of the workers and peasants"; their respective functions are clearly demarcated: the union must, above all else, see to it that the factory—the fundamental unit of society for which the union is so-to-speak politically and morally responsible—

achieves and, if possible, exceeds the target set by the state planners.

The members of the FDGB are not free to express their opinions; they have no right of co-determination and no influence on the wage structure or working conditions; nor are they in a position to employ the unions' traditional methods of militancy, i.e. strikes. The Labour Code of 1961, which applies throughout the German Democratic Republic, shows clearly that the individual can no longer choose or determine the amount or nature of the work he does.

The curtailment of the workers' rights, which in fact amounts to a loss of self-determination, is justified by the fiction of the identity of interests of the workers and the state. According to this argument the management of the state and the society is in the hands of the workers' representatives and this guarantees that the workers' interests are directly represented; moreover, since all enterprises are "nationally owned" they are in the hands of the workers themselves; in a "workers' and peasants' state" no conflict can thus ever arise between the political leaders and the workers. An important factor in this system of political and ideological dependence is the "socialist work morale", which, as Ulbricht stated at the SED's 5th Congress in 1958, "lies at the very heart of all the moral relationships of the socialist society". He calls it the Seventh Commandment of "socialist morality". The Labour Code of 1961 states that "every working person has the duty to maintain socialist labour discipline; this is a basic rule which applies to everyone who works; in particular he must protect and increase socialist property".

To understand these ideological embellishments and the reality which lies behind them, we must first realize to what extent the social structure of the German Democratic Republic has changed in the last twenty years. New social classes have emerged while old ones are either much reduced or have disappeared altogether; private ownership of the means of production has been almost completely abolished; nearly 95 per cent of the working population are dependent for their employment, and in 90 per cent of the cases the state is the employer.

The main features of the social and economic developments

in the German Democratic Republic are determined by the same modern, highly industrialized production methods as those in the German Federal Republic, and tend to resemble closely the trends observed there. In both there is a growth of the tertiary sector of employment, diminishing employment figures and an increased tendency to mechanization in agriculture and a preference for technical as against service occupations. There is little difference in wage structures between West and East Germany, i.e. the wage scales of different industries and the scale of average wages are very much the same in both regions. But the majority of workers in the German Federal Republic receive higher wages than the workers in the German Democratic Republic (the difference is about 10–12 per cent), quite apart from the difference in purchasing power. A small group of East German workers employed in iron and uranium mining receives exceptionally high wages not equalled anywhere in the Federal Republic. A special difficulty with which the German Democratic Republic has to contend is the comparatively high average age of the working population and the proportion of women workers which is greater than in the Federal Republic. This reduces the general working potential.

During the last few years the attitude of the workers to the "workers' and peasants' state" has been increasingly one of accommodation to the prevailing political conditions and of making the best possible use of what is economically feasible. Such objective data as are available indicate that the workers' attitude to the state and the party are not influenced by the fact that undertakings are nationally owned and "belong to the workers"; the workers tend to think of the state and the party as something apart. With good ideological reason the SED has artificially fostered the workers' self-confidence by acknowledging that their qualifications make them indispensable. This has given the industrial workers a very realistic estimate of their own position; they realize that in a very well defined sense the Ulbricht state depends on the 3·65 million workers who are employed in industry, building and transport.

An essential factor which influences the workers' outlook in East Germany is the collective solidarity of small groups of workers, developed in their pursuit of material interests. The way in which production in nationally owned enterprises is organized encourages this solidarity. In this instance too the system has had an effect which was never intended. The small group acquires a solidarity which militates against the required direct identification with the interests of the whole community and which conflicts with the formal organization of the enterprise. Identification with a small group of workmates leads to a loss of political involvement and offers some protection against uncomfortable social and political pressures. The wish to escape such pressures—quite apart from the desire for personal advancement— leads to frequent changes of employment.

The SED as well as the FDGB whose main task is "political persuasion" on the shop floor, try to counteract this tendency towards group-identification and fluctuation by fostering social and cultural activities at places of work in the spirit of the slogan : "Work together, learn together, live together"; but so far their attempts have failed.

> The young people in the German Democratic Republic also show a growing desire to live a life of their own ... But they lay more stress on their work than do the young citizens of the Federal Republic; and this implies a greater feeling of responsibility, a more serious outlook on life, and, because of the social system in East Germany, a not inconsiderable orientation towards the collective.

In general, the attitudes and outlook of the workers in the German Democratic Republic are not merely a symptom of opposition to social norms imposed by the régime or of loyalty to the traditional norms of a society such as existed before 1945; it is rather the case that modern industrial production methods tend to foster a certain objectivity, to debunk ideologies and to reactivate the personal aspects of social relations.

Hence it would be wrong to regard the ruling party's influence on society and social relations as wholly destructive and obstructive. The SED has frequently initiated, stimulated and eventually consolidated new social norms which were made necessary by modern industrial production methods (and by the economic difficulties peculiar to the German Democratic Republic); e.g. by assuming the role of "exponent of technical progress" or by introducing "socialist competition" it improved the workers' professional status and allowed their social prestige to rise; to a limited extent it has thus brought about a correspondence between its own norms and those of society. Certain pressures such as its very real economic dependence on the industrial workers seem to be forcing the SED to redefine its models and norms so that they accord more closely with the changes in society. It is too early to say whether and to what extent this will affect its political ideology and practice. Equally unpredictable is the ideological and political effect of the gradual reduction in the number of so-called productive workers; this "class-conscious section of the working class"—Lenin's "real proletarians"—is being eroded by technological changes, particularly in engineering. The social effects of automation present another problem with which the German Democratic Republic will eventually have to come to grips.

The Christian Labour Movement in Germany

(Summary of the Chapters on the above subject in the
German edition of the book)

1. Before 1914

Serious concern with social questions among both Catholics
and Protestants preceded the beginnings of denominational
Christian Workers' Associations. In catholic circles this concern becomes manifest at an earlier stage than in the protestant community. In 1848 events of importance in this respect
occurred in both denominations: the agenda of the Catholic
Congress held that year at Mainz included for the first time
a discussion on the social evils and abuses which accompanied
the rise of industrial capitalism; on the protestant side, *J. H.
Wichern* (1808–1881) founded the Home Mission (*Innere
Mission*)—as distinct from overseas Missions—to counter some
of these abuses. The remedies were sought in religious instruc-
tion, moral exhortation and charity, rather than in social
reform or a change in the system of society such as were
advocated by the pioneers of the socialist labour movement.

The formation of the first Catholic Journeymen's and
Catholic Workers' Associations goes back to the middle of the
nineteenth century. But it was not till 1869 that a programme
emerged round which catholic workers could rally. An important speech made that year by *Wilhelm Emmanuel Ketteler*,
Bishop of Mainz (1811–1877), became their *Magna Charta*.
This pronouncement heralded the change in the Catholics'
attitude towards support for social reforms. It included
demands for higher wages, shorter hours, laws against child
labour and for the protection of working mothers. Later, the
social policy evolved by the Centre Party (*Zentrum*), a party
founded in 1870 to defend catholic interests threatened by
Bismarck's *Kulturkampf*, reflected the impact of Ketteler and
his ideas.

In 1877 the first candidate sponsored by the Catholic Workers' Movement—a worker—was elected to Parliament. In 1889 there were 280 Catholic Workers' Associations, with more than 60,000 members.

The first Protestant Workers' Associations, led by clergymen, were founded in 1882. By 1890 they had been consolidated, working mainly for better relations between workers and employers. The Protestant Church with its conservative, patriarchal outlook was unable to respond to the challenge of the first Industrial Revolution. It is true that *Adolf Stöcker* (1835–1909) and the Christian-Social Workers' Party (*Christlich-soziale Arbeiterpartei*), which he founded in 1878, advocated social reforms within the existing political system. However, the main aim of these activities was to keep the workers in the Protestant Church and loyal to the Prussian monarchy. The party thus became an electoral arm of the Conservatives. As a general rule the Protestant Workers' Associations showed themselves to be more subservient to conservative interests than their catholic counterparts.

After 1890, a group of Protestants, led by *Friedrich Naumann* (1860–1919) and opposed to Stöcker, became active. This group realized that the workers wanted to act on their own behalf rather than be mere objects of charity or social policy. In 1897 Naumann, despairing of the possibility that his Church might make any real contribution towards solving the social question, renounced his office in the Church. However, with only one representative in Parliament, this group attained little influence and was dissolved in 1903.

It is important to note here that certain sections of the workers belonging to the Protestant Church, or professing its faith, were attracted to the Social Democratic Party and the Free Trade Unions and therefore remained unresponsive to the recruiting efforts of the various protestant groups. Catholic workers supported the christian political and trade-union organizations in much larger numbers.

The Catholic Workers' Associations, also led by priests, were given a new impetus by the encyclical *Rerum Novarum* of *Pope Leo XIII* (1810–1903), issued in 1891. This contained the theological justification for the catholic criticism of the capitalist system and for the social and political implications affecting the catholic organizations. The basic guide on social questions provided by *Rerum Novarum* was reinforced in 1931 by the encyclical *Quadragesimo Anno* of *Pope Pius XI* (1857–1939).

By 1914 the Catholic Workers' Associations had a membership of 500,000. They did not at first assume any trade-union functions, nor were they engaged in political action. Nevertheless they helped to prepare catholic workers for these broader tasks.

The year 1899 marked an important new departure for workers of both denominations. It saw the foundation of the Confederation of Christian Trade Unions which included both Catholic and Protestant Workers' Associations. *Adam Stegerwald* (1874–1945), elected General Secretary in 1903, organized the Confederation on the model of the Free Trade Unions. From 18,000 members in 1899, it grew to 250,000 in 1907, and 351,000 in 1912 (in round figures).

The view that for trade-union activities an inter-denominational basis and lay leaders were preferable had gradually gained ground. The Catholic Congresses of 1896, 1898 and 1899 had approved the establishment of christian trade unions as a complement to denominational workers' associations. But this development was opposed by certain sections of the Catholic Church which were unwilling to abandon exclusive control and priests as leaders. They were not satisfied with the fact that the Catholics were always the dominant element in the Christian Trade Unions, both numerically and in other respects. In fighting the resistance of some of their own Church leaders, the catholic workers, while building up the Christian Trade Unions, achieved a certain degree of emancipation from clerical authority.

The Protestant Church showed no opposition to inter-denominational unions. This did not reflect broadmindedness of outlook, but rather a general indifference to the problems of the industrial workers.

2. *1918–1945*

In the period of the Weimar Republic the activities of the Catholic Workers' Associations increased. From the start, they were in favour of the republic, and they also demanded a new economic and social order in which more account would be taken of the workers' interests. In 1928 they joined the Catholic Workers' International, whose first congress that year endorsed far-reaching social aims such as a guaranteed right to co-determination for the workers in industry, account-ability of entrepreneurs, parity of representation for trade unions on public economic bodies, economic planning and a fairer distribution of the national product. There can be no doubt that the Catholics formed the Left wing of the Christian Trade Unions.

Membership in the Christian Trade Unions rose from 1 million in 1919 to 1·1 million in 1920, but by 1931 it had fallen to 0·69 million. However, in the industrial heart of Rhineland-Westphalia they remained a strong force.

Politically, the Christian Trade Unions found support in the (catholic) Centre Party on the one hand, and in the re-constituted (conservative) German National People's Party (*Deutschnationale Volkspartei*) on the other. Attempts to secure their own parliamentary representation failed because the Catholic Workers' Associations refused to abandon the Centre Party in which their influence had steadily risen since 1918. Yet—except in Prussia—the Centre Party moved to the Right. The political aim pursued by such national leaders as Adam Stegerwald was to rally the forces of the Right in an attempt to stem the disintegration of the Weimar Republic. This policy met with the opposition of Left-wing catholic trade-union leaders like *Jakob Kaiser* (1888–1961) and *Karl Arnold* (1901–1958). Although the Centre Party suffered a loss of votes to the Social Democratic and Communist Parties in the 1928 elections, its unity was maintained. It was not shaken even in 1931 when the Government of *Brüning* (b. 1885), himself a former trade-union official, introduced very retrograde social measures which were only slightly modified by pressure from the Christian Trade Unions.

On the Protestant side, after 1918, the leaders of the workers' movement and of the Christian-social group which adhered to the Stöcker tradition joined forces with the recon-stituted party of the Conservatives. But in 1929 the reaction-ary policies pursued by this party under its leader Hugenberg

caused such revulsion among the protestant workers' representatives that they resigned from the party. Their efforts to
form an independent group in Parliament were unsuccessful;
they lacked sufficient support, even after the large German
National Shop Assistants' Union (*Deutschnationaler Hand-
lungsgehilfenverband*), a notorious Right-wing body, had
joined them. Many members of this union supported Hitler
as early as 1930.

Most of the organized catholic workers were against the
National Socialists. In the last years of the Weimar Republic
they tried to counter the terrorism of the extreme Right as
well as of the Left. But Centre Party and Catholic Church
leaders, like other groups, failed to grasp the true nature of
the coming Hitler régime, partly because they were so
obsessed with the Bolshevist menace from which Hitler
promised to save Germany. They left their followers wholly
unprepared for the Nazi holocaust.

The record of the Christian Trade Unions includes some
sharp attacks against Hitler and his party; they also supported such steps as the "Schleicher Experiment" in order to
avert the threat of Hitler. Yet the slogans about a strong
national state which Hitler alone could create had a certain
appeal for them. Moreover, like the Free Trade Unions, they
entertained the vain hope that tactical manoeuvres might
secure their survival. Early in 1933 the Christian Trade
Unions offered Hitler their co-operation. A few months later
they were integrated into the German Labour Front and their
leaders denounced as "traitors to the National Revolution".
Nor did the Catholic Workers' Associations have a chance
of survival, although their central organization was not
banned till 1936. The Ketteler House in Cologne became the
centre of the catholic workers' resistance. Many resistance
leaders came from the ranks of the catholic workers'
organizations and from among protestant workers. Some came
even from the Shop Assistants' Union after it had been
dissolved.

3. After 1945

After 1945, an inter-denominational christian party was set
up under Adenauer's leadership, the Christian Democratic

Union (*Christlich-demokratische Union*—CDU)[1], on the new model followed in several countries of post-war Europe. The Christian Trade Unions, on the other hand, were not resurrected, though the Catholic Workers' Associations were re-activated. These soon reached a membership of 400,000 and took upon themselves extensive tasks in the fields of education and training. Their influence was felt at the Catholic Congresses. Thus, e.g. the Congress held in 1949 pronounced in favour of co-determination of the workers in industry as a "natural right in a God-given social order."

In 1949, a united trade-union organization on a non-party basis was set up. This new venture was strongly supported by the Catholic Workers' Associations. Later, however, some Catholics came to favour a return to separate christian unions. Such unions were in fact set up in 1955 (without as yet becoming very important), mainly on the insistence of the Christian Trade Union International which would otherwise have had no affiliate in Germany.

In the newly constituted CDU, the progressive forces of Catholicism contributed a great deal to the shaping of the social policy of the Federal Republic during its first two decades.

The Protestant Workers' Associations were also revived after the war; in 1952 they joined together in the Protestant Workers' Movement of Germany. Although traditionalist in religious matters and politically inclined to conservatism, they supported the united trade-union movement from the start, as did the Protestant Church itself in spite of the fact that the Social Democrats were the dominant element in the movement. This support continued even after the re-establishment of christian unions.

A number of other protestant organizations and institutions which were set up in the post-war years developed a distinctly progressive outlook, attuned to the conditions of the modern industrial age. Three of them are particularly worthy of mention : Workers' Action (*Arbeiterwerk*), which, apart from trying to act as a spiritual adviser to industrial workers, provides educational opportunities for them; the Adult Education

[1] The Bavarian sister organization is the Christian Social Union (*Christlich-soziale Union*—CSU).

Colleges (*Sozialakademien*), which give protestant workers a forward-looking social orientation, provide training and also encourage mutual aid; the Co-ordinating Committee on Labour Questions (*Aktionsgemeinschaft für Arbeiterfragen*), which tries to ensure co-operation among all protestant bodies catering for the needs of industrial workers.

4. Christian versus Socialist Ideas

In the middle of the 19th century the ideas of Marx and Lassalle made a strong impact on German Catholics who were concerned with social issues. The challenge presented by the labour leaders' criticism of the capitalist system could not be ignored. In fact, socialist attacks on the class society have never ceased to be a challenge to christian communities.

On the other hand, in its basic outlook and aims, Social Democracy with its tenets on ownership, the role of the class struggle and the materialist conception of history was incompatible with catholic convictions relating to property, the guild system and, later, the corporate structure of society as evolved in Papal encyclicals. Nor could the Thomist view of "natural rights", which influenced much of catholic social doctrine, be reconciled with socialist concepts.

Despite these differences, agreement was possible in the realm of concrete measures: social policy, labour legislation, specific trade-union demands. Yet at the same time both the Catholics and the Protestants continued their relentless struggle against Socialism through their respective political and industrial organizations. This struggle was inspired and guided by the Churches. Hostility often went so far as to deny the socialist movement its ethical motivation. The advent of Hitler put an end to this bitter fight, although under Adenauer it still reverberated in electoral campaigning.

The Social Democrats' view of society was secular; science was everything, religion, for most of them, outdated. The Churches were regarded as allies of their enemies, the ruling classes. It is true that the social-democratic programme declared religion to be a matter of individual conscience, and that religious socialists could work within the party for their beliefs. But the Freethinkers' Organization was most influential in party circles.

Developments since 1945, in the Social Democratic Party as well as in the Catholic and Protestant Churches, have radically changed the situation. Today the Social Democrats regard modern catholic concepts of social and political life as compatible with their own new programme, adopted at Godesberg in 1959. In their view such differences as still remain are not insuperable. The striking gains of the Social Democratic Party in strongholds of the Catholics in the elections of recent years bear this out. In North-Rhine Westphalia the Catholics have now even abandoned their stubborn defence of the denominational school system. All the same, many Catholics still insist that the fundamental gulf has not disappeared.

Protestantism, since 1945, has become more aware of social reality, more open to the need for changes in society. Consequently its attitude to democratic Socialism has ceased to be hostile. The theoretical concepts of the Godesberg Programme are close to protestant social ethics. Protestant opinion in Germany has been deeply influenced by the ideas of the "responsible society" first put forward by the World Council of Churches in Amsterdam in 1948, and developed at subsequent conferences of the World Council.

SELECTED BIBLIOGRAPHY
FOR THE NEW ENGLISH EDITION
(revised by the Author)

Adler, Victor, *Briefwechsel mit August Bebel und Karl Kautsky,* Vienna, 1954.

Angress, Werner T., *Stillborn Revolution,* Princeton, 1963.

Bahne, Siegfried, *Die KPD und das Ende von Weimar: das Scheitern einer Politik 1932 – 1935,* Frankfurt/New York, 1976.

Balser, Frolinde, 'Sozial-Demokratie 1848/49 – 1863. Die erste deutsche Arbeiterorganisation "Allgemeine Arbeiterverbrüderung" nach der Revolution', *Industrielle Welt,* vol.2, Munich, 1960.

Braunthal, Gerard, *Der Allgemeine Deutsche Gewerkschaftsbund. Zur Politik der Arbeiterbewegung in der Weimarer Republik,* Cologne, 1981.

Braunthal, Julius, *Geschichte der Internationale,* 3 vols., Hanover, 1961 – 3; 2nd ed., Bonn/Bad Godesberg, 1978 (transl. as *History of the International,* London, 1967).

Bry, Gerhard, *Wages in Germany, 1871 – 1945,* Princeton, NJ, 1960.

Carsten, Francis L., *War against War. British and German Radical Movements in the First World War,* London, 1982.

Comfort, Richard A., *Revolutionary Hamburg: Labor Politics in the Early Weimar Republic,* Stanford, Calif., 1966.

Crew, David F., *Town in the Ruhr. A social history of Bochum, 1860 – 1914,* New York, 1979.

Dowe, D., 'The Workers' Choral Movement before the First World War', in *Journal of Contemporary History,* vol.13, 1978, pp. 269 – 96.

Drechsler, Hanno, *Die Sozialistische Arbeiterpartei Deutschlands (SAPD). Ein Beitrag zur Geschichte der deutschen Arbeiterbewegung am Ende der Weimarer Republik,* Meisenheim, 1965.

Edinger, Lewis J., *German Exile Politics. The Social Democratic Executive Committee in the Nazi Era*, Berkeley/Los Angeles, 1956.

—, *Kurt Schumacher — a Study in Personality and Political Behaviour*, Stanford, Calif., 1965.

Evans, Richard J., *The German Working Class, 1888 – 1933*, Totowa, NJ, 1982.

— (ed.), *Society and Politics in Wilhelmine Germany*, London, 1978.

Feldman, Gerald D., *Army, Industry and Labor in Germany, 1914 – 1918*, Princeton, NJ, 1966.

Fetscher, Iring, *Der Marxismus. Seine Geschichte in Dokumenten*: vol.1, *Philosophie, Ideologie;* vol.2, *Oekonomie, Soziologie;* vol.3, *Politik*, Munich, 1962 et seq.

Fischer, Wolfram, *Armut in der Geschichte. Erscheinungsformen und Lösungsversuche der 'sozialen Frage' in Europa seit dem Mittelalter*, Göttingen, 1982.

Flechtheim, Ossip K., *Die KPD in der Weimarer Republik*, Frankfurt, 1976.

Fromm, Erich, *The Working Class in Weimar Germany. A Psychological and Sociological Study*, Leamington Spa, 1984.

Gay, Peter, *The Dilemma of Democratic Socialism. Eduard Bernstein's Challenge to Marx*, New York, 1952.

Geary, Dick, *European Labour Protest, 1848 – 1939*, London, 1981.

Grebing, Helga, *Der Revisionismus: von Bernstein bis zum 'Prager Frühling'*, Munich, 1977.

—, *Arbeiterbewegung. Sozialer Protest und Kollektive Interessenvertretung bis 1914*, Munich, 1985.

— (ed.), *Fritz Sternberg (1895 – 1963)*, Frankfurt, 1981.

Groh, Dieter, *Negative Integration und revolutionärer Attentismus. Die deutsche Sozialdemokratie am Vorabend des Ersten Weltkrieges*, Frankfurt/Berlin/Vienna, 1973.

Guttsman, W.L. *The German Social Democratic Party, 1875 – 1933. From Ghetto to Government*, London, 1981.

Hall, H.A., 'By Other Means, The Legal Struggle against the SPD in Wilhelmine Germany, 1890 – 1900', in *Historical Journal*, vol.17, 1974, pp. 365 – 86.

—, 'The War of Words. The Anti-Socialist Offensive in Germany', in *Journal of Modern History*, Vol. 11, nos 2 – 3, 1976, pp. 15 – 32.

Haupt, Georges, *Socialism and the Great War: The Collapse of the Second International,* Oxford, 1972.

Heckart, B., *From Bassermann to Bebel. The 'Grand Bloc's' Quest for Reform in the Kaiserreich, 1900–1914,* New Haven, Conn., 1974.

Hunt, Richard, *German Social Democracy 1918–1933,* New Haven, Conn., 1972.

Joll, James, *The Second International,* London, 1975.

Kaden, Albrecht, *Einheit oder Freiheit. Die Wiedergründung der SPD 1945–46,* Hanover, 1964.

Kautsky, K., *Social Revolution,* Chicago, 1902.

Klotzbach, Kurt, *Der Weg zur Staatspartei: Programmatik, praktische Politik und Organisation der deutschen Sozialdemokratie, 1945 bis 1965,* Berlin, 1982.

Kluth, Hans, *Die KPD in der Bundesrepublik. Ihre politische Tätigkeit und Organisation 1945–1956,* Cologne, 1959.

Kocka, Jürgen, *Lohnarbeit und Klassenbildung. Arbeiter und Arbeiterbewegung in Deutschland 1800–1875,* Berlin/Bonn, 1983.

—, *Facing Total War. German Society 1914–1918,* Leamington Spa, 1984.

Kolb, Eberhard, *Die Arbeiterräte in der deutschen Innenpolitik 1918 bis 1919,* Düsseldorf, 1962.

Kotowski, Georg, *Friedrich Ebert. Eine politische Biographie.* Vol. 1, *Der Aufstieg eines deutschen Arbeiterführers 1871–1917,* Wiesbaden 1963.

Kühne, Karl, *Ökonomie und Marxismus.* Vol.1, *Zur Renaissance des Marxschen Systems;* vol.2, *Zur Dynamik des Marxschen Systems,* Neuwied, 1972, 1974.

Langewiesche, Dieter, and Schönhoven, Klaus (eds.), *Arbeiter in Deutschland. Studien zur Lebensweise der Arbeiterschaft im Zeitalter der Industrialisierung,* Paderborn, 1981.

Lidtke, Vernon L., *The Outlawed Party,* Princeton, NJ, 1966.

—, 'Songs of the German Labor Movement, 1864–1914', unpublished paper. (A German version has appeared in *Geschichte und Gesellschaft 5,* No. 1 (1979), pp. 54–82.)

Lassalle, Ferdinand, *Eine Auswahl für unsere Zeit,* ed. by Helmut Hirsch, Frankfurt, 1963.

Liebknecht, Wilhelm, *Briefwechsel mit Karl Marx und Friedrich*

Engels, ed. by Georg Eckert, The Hague, 1963.

Link, Werner, *Die Geschichte des Internationalen Jugend-Bundes (IJB) und des Internationalen Sozialistischen Kampf-Bundes (ISK). Ein Beitrag zur Geschichte der Arbeiterbewegung in der Weimarer Republik und im Dritten Reich,* Meisenheim, 1964.

Luthardt, Wolfgang, (ed.), *Sozialdemokratische Arbeiterbewegung und Weimarer Republik. Materialien zur gesellschaftlichen Entwicklung 1927–1933,* 2 vols. Frankfurt, 1978.

Marx, Karl, *A Contribution to the Critique of Political Economy,* rev. ed., London, 1964.

—, *Capital,* vols. I–II, Intro. by G. H. Cole, London, 1929.

—, *Frühe Schriften,* vol. 1, ed. by Hans-Joachim Lieber and Peter Furth, Stuttgart, 1962.

—, and Friedrich Engels, *Communist Manifesto,* Intro. by Harold J. Laski, London, 1947.

Matthias, Erich, *Sozialdemokratie und Nation. Zur Ideengeschichte der sozialdemokratischen Emigration 1933–1938,* Stuttgart, 1952.

—, *Kautsky und der Kautskyanismus,* Tübingen, 1957.

—, and Rudolf Morsey, *Das Ende der Parteien 1933,* Düsseldorf, 1979.

Meyer, Thomas, *Bernsteins Konstruktiver Sozialismus,* Berlin, 1977.

—, and Horst Heimann (eds.), *Reformsozialismus und Sozialdemokratie: Zur Theoriediskussion des demokratischen Sozialismus in der Weimarer Republik,* Berlin, 1982.

Miller, Susanne, *Das Problem der Freiheit im Sozialismus. Freiheit, Staat und Revolution in der Programmatik der Sozialdemokratie von Lassalle bis zum Revisionismusstreit,* 2nd ed., Frankfurt, 1974.

—, *Burgfrieden oder Klassenkampf. Die deutsche Sozialdemokratie im Ersten Weltkrieg,* Düsseldorf, 1976.

—, *Die Bürde der Macht. Die deutsche Sozialdemokratie 1918–1920,* Düsseldorf, 1978.

Moore, Barrington, *Injustice: The Social Bases of Obedience and Revolt,* New York, 1978.

Morgan, David W., *The Socialist Left and the German Revolution. A History of the Independent Social Democratic Party, 1917–1922,* Ithaca, NY, 1975.

Morgan, R., *The German Social Democrats and the First*

International, 1864–1872, Cambridge, 1965.

Moses, John A., *Trade Unionism in Germany from Bismarck to Hitler 1869–1933,* 2 vols, London, 1982.

Nettl, Peter, *Rosa Luxemburg,* London, 1969.

—, 'The German Social Democratic Party 1890–1914 as a Political Model', in *Past & Present,* no. 30, 1965, pp. 29–95.

Neumann, Sigmund, *Die deutschen Parteien. Wesen und Wandel nach dem Kriege,* Berlin, 1932; repr. as *Die Parteien der Weimarer Republik,* Stuttgart, 1965.

Niethammer, Lutz, Ulrich Borsdorf and Peter Brandt (eds.), *Arbeiterinitiative 1945. Antifaschistische Ausschüsse und Reorganisation der Arbeiterbewegung in Deutschland,* Wuppertal, 1976.

Nolan, Mary, *Social Democracy and Society. Working-class Radicalism in Düsseldorf, 1890–1920,* Cambridge, 1981.

Oertzen, Peter von, *Betriebsräte in der Novemberrevolution,* Düsseldorf, 1963.

Offermann, Toni, *Arbeiterbewegung und liberales Bürgertum in Deutschland 1850–1863,* Bonn, 1979.

Osterroth, Franz, and Dieter Schuster, *Chronik der deutschen Sozialdemokratie:* vol.1, *Bis zum Ende des Ersten Weltkrieges;* vol.2, *Vom Beginn der Weimarer Republik bis zum Ende des Zweiten Weltkrieges;* vol.3, *Nach dem Zweiten Weltrieg,* 2nd ed., Berlin/Bonn, 1978.

Pirker, Theo, *Die SPD nach Hitler. Die Geschichte der Sozialdemokratischen Partei Deutschlands 1945–1964,* Munich, 1964.

Preller, Ludwig, *Sozialpolitik in der Weimarer Republik,* Stuttgart, 1949; repr. Kronberg, Düsseldorf, 1978.

Ritter, Gerhard A., *Die Arbeiterbewegung im Wilhelminischen Reich. Die Sozialdemokratische Partei und die freien Gewerkschaften 1890–1900,* 2nd ed., Berlin, 1963.

—, *Staat, Arbeiterschaft und Arbeiterbewegung in Deutschland, Vom Vormärz bis zum Ende der Weimarer Republik,* Berlin/Bonn, 1982.

—, 'Workers' Culture in Imperial Germany', in *Journal of Contemporary History,* vol. 13, 1978, pp. 165–89.

Rosenberg, Arthur, *A History of the German Republic,* London, 1936 (New York, 1965).

—, *Entstehung der Weimarer Republik,* Frankfurt, 1961.

Roth, Günther, *The Social Democrats in Imperial Germany. A study in working-class isolation and national integration,* Totowa, NJ 1963.

Ryder, A.J., *The German Revolution of 1918,* Cambridge, 1967.

Saul, Klaus, Jens Flemming, Dirk Stegmann and Peter-Christian Witt (eds.), *Arbeiterfamilien im Kaiserreich: Materialien zur Sozialgeschichte in Deutschland 1871–1914,* Königstein/Taunus, 1982.

Schieder, Wolfgang, 'Anfänge der deutschen Arbeiterbewegung. Die Auslandsvereine im Jahrzehnt nach der Julirevolution von 1830', *Industrielle Welt,* vol.4, Stuttgart 1963.

Schneider, Michael, *Aussperrung. Ihre Geschichte und Funktion vom Kaiserreich bis heute,* Frankfurt, 1980.

—, *Die christlichen Gewerkschaften 1894–1933,* Bonn, 1982.

Schofer, Lawrence, *The Formation of a Modern Labor Force. Upper Silesia, 1865–1914,* Berkeley, 1975.

Schönhoven, Klaus, and Erich Matthias (eds.), *Solidarität und Menschenwürde. Etappen der deutschen Gewerkschaftsgeschichte von den Anfängen bis zur Gegenwart,* Bonn, 1984.

Schorske, Carl E., *German Social Democracy, 1905–1917: The Development of the Great Schism,* new ed., New York, 1972.

Schraepler, Ernst, *Quellen zur Geschichte der sozialen Frage in Deutschland:* vol.1, *1800–1870;* vol.2, *1871 bis zur Gegenwart,* Göttingen, 1955, 1957.

Schulze, Hagen, *Otto Braun oder Preussens demokratische Sendung. Eine Biographie,* Frankfurt, 1977.

Snell, J., 'The German Socialists in the Last Imperial Reichstag', in *Bulletin of the International Insitute for Social History,* vol.7, 1952, pp.196–205.

Stearns, Peter, *European Society in Upheaval,* London, 1967.

—, *Lives of Labor: Work in Maturing Industrial Society,* New York, 1975.

Steinberg, Hans-Josef, *Sozialismus und deutsche Sozialdemokratie. Zur Ideologie der Partei vor dem Ersten Weltkrieg,* Hanover, 1967.

Tampke, Jürgen, *The Ruhr and Revolution,* London, 1979.

Tenfelde, Klaus, and Heinrich Volkmann (eds.), *Streik. Zur*

Geschichte des Arbeitskampfes in Deutschland während der Industrialisierung, Munich, 1981.

Tennstedt, Florian, *Sozialgeschichte der Sozialpolitik in Deutschland, Vom 18. Jahrhundert bis zum Ersten Weltkrieg*, Göttingen, 1981.

Thonessen, W., *The Emancipation of Women: The Rise and Decline of the Women's Movement in German Social Democracy, 1863–1933*, London, 1973.

Tilly, Richard, 'Popular Disturbances in Nineteenth-Century Germany', in *Journal of Social History*, vol.4, 1970, pp. 1–40.

Timm, Helga, *Die deutsche Sozialpolitik und der Bruch der großen Koalition im März 1930*, Düsseldorf, 1952, repr. 1982.

Tjaden, Karl H., *Struktur und Funktion der 'KPD-Opposition' (KPO). Eine organisationssoziologische Untersuchung zur 'Rechts'-Opposition im deutschen Kommunismus zur Zeit der Weimarer Republik*, Meisenheim, 1964.

Vranicki, Predag, *Geschichte des Marxismus*, 2 vols., Frankfurt, 1972, 1974.

Waldmann, Eric, *The Spartacist Uprising of 1919*, Milwaukee, 1958.

Weber, Hermann, (ed.) *Der deutsche Kommunismus. Dokumente*, Cologne, 1963.

Wheeler, Robert F., 'The Independent Social Democrats and the Internationals', unpubl. diss., Pittsburgh, 1970.

Winkler, Heinrich August, *Von der Revolution zur Stabilisierung. Arbeiter und Arbeiterbewegung in der Weimarer Republik 1918–1924*, Bonn, 1984.

Zwahr, Hartmut, *Zur Konstituierung des Proletariats als Klasse. Strukturuntersuchungen über das Leipziger Proletariat während der industriellen Revolution*, Munich, 1981.

INDEX OF NAMES